Choosing Color for Logos & Packaging

RotoVision

A RotoVision Book

Published and distributed by RotoVision SA
Route Suisse 9
CH-1295 Mies
Switzerland

RotoVision SA
Sales and Editorial Office
Sheridan House, 114 Western Road
Hove BN3 1DD, UK

Tel: +44 (0)1273 72 72 68
Fax: +44 (0)1273 72 72 69
www.rotovision.com

10 9 8 7 6 5 4 3 2 1

ISBN: 978-2-88893-095-2

Art direction: Tony Seddon
Design and layout: Lisa Båtsvik-Miller

Typeset in Trade Gothic Light

Reprographics in Singapore by ProVision Pte.
Tel: +65 6334 7720
Fax: +65 6334 7721

Printed in China by
1010 Printing International Ltd.

We would like to thank all those who have contributed to
and made this book possible. So many people have shown
generosity and insight that it is impossible to list them all.
Our deepest gratitude goes to:

Christine Pickett for making us sound like geniuses;
Tanya Ortega and Carlo Irigoyen for their help in the international
call for entries; the International Council of Graphic Design Association
(ICOGRADA) and the American Institute of Graphic Arts (AIGA) for
supporting the call; Danny Giang, Jimmy Khemthong, and Maho Sasai
for their help; all our students, who have inspired us to think differently;
the people at RotoVision, especially Lindy Dunlop and Tony Seddon for
their continued support; and finally, everyone who answered the call
and may or may not appear in this book—it would not have been
possible without your participation.

Choosing Color for Logos & Packaging

Solutions for 2D & 3D designs

John T. Drew &
Sarah A. Meyer

For our daughters, Olivia and Gustava,
who have shown tremendous patience;
Frank and Elaine Meyer (grandparents
of our daughters); Colonel Mark C. Bane Jr.,
their great-grandfather; and the late great
Mark C. Bane III, their great-uncle.

CONTENTS

Logos: 2D Designs

Not only does color have a definite effect on readability and legibility of text, it also has associated behavioral effects. The dynamics of practical color use, in print-based, motion, and interactive graphics, are intrinsic to successful graphic design. This collection of visually stimulating design demonstrates the color issues involved in logo and 2D design today.

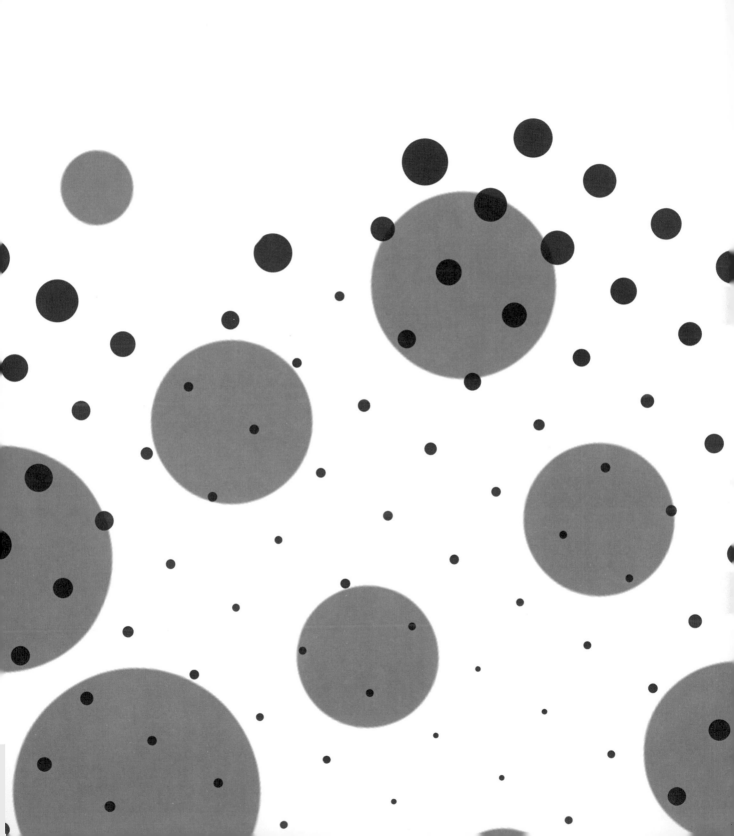

One Color

The world's best logomarks, logotypes, and simple symbols are designed first as a one-color mark. Color sells a product. The term "one-color mark" may seem like an oxymoron, but think of it as a matter of versatility. Logos should work in any given situation, whether being transmitted by fax or being seen on the Web. From the initial sketch to the finished mark, versatility must always be a primary objective. The logo objectives should be applied not only to color, shape, form, tone, and texture, but also to the context for branding purposes. Objectives should include any foreseen and unforeseen budgetary constraints.

It is a tall order to predict how a mark will be used in the future, but logomarks, logotypes, and simple symbols have longevity like no other graphic-design product. If designed correctly, a mark will stand the test of time. Through careful observation, research, and knowledge of color management, a logo can be passed down from generation to generation, no matter the business or corporation.

UNITED AFRICAN COMPANIES

Studio: Essex Two

Associative Color Response:
• black: prestigious, strong

Color Scheme: one hue

In this logomark, a modular system consisting of three shapes that are rotated and repeated three times is an excellent way of constructing a mark with a corporate feel.

THE MAZING SHOW

Designer: Art Chantry

Associative Color Response:
• black: percussive, expressive

Color Scheme: one hue

This expressive logotype is carried out through the manipulation of font, the constellation of letterforms, and the choice of typeface. These three factors combined add up to a playfully expressive mark. In most cases the look and feel of a logotype is established by the font/ fonts used—font choice is almost always the primary signifier.

MUDHONEY

Designer: Art Chantry

Associative Color Response:
• black: mysterious

Color Scheme: one hue

The manipulation of font and placement creates an energetic mark that represents a crazed madness. Today any letterform or font can be converted into vector art. This ability gives designers tremendous flexibility to create logotypes that are unique and relate to the subject matter.

SMASH HITS

Designer: Art Chantry

Associative Color Response:
• black: anger, fear, nightmares

Color Scheme: one hue

The manipulation of letterforms creates a metaphor that is both expressive and direct. In almost all cases, texture creates a visual magnet, pulling in the reader to discover additional content-based information.

G FORCE SNOWBOARDS

Designer: Art Chantry

Associative Color Response:
• black: heavy, basic

Color Scheme: one hue

Here the interplay between font, texture, and placement creates a dynamic mark that is carried out through simile. Note how the letterforms in "force" progressively collide into and overlap each another. The texture found in the mark creates motion from left to right.

JOE JUNK

Designer/Illustrator: Lanny Sommese

Associative Color Response:
• black: powerful, mysterious

Color Scheme: one hue with gray tones— conveyed through line work

Substitution is one of the most powerful tools a designer can use to create an effective logomark or logotype. The scale at which substitution is used should relate directly to content. In this case, a huge amount of substitution is used in order to convey the idea of junk.

HÜSKER DÜ

Designer: Art Chantry

Associative Color Response:
• black: despairing, depressing

Color Scheme: one hue with gray tones— conveyed through line work

This simile-based manipulation is created through the use of texture and distortion. Texture is used, through line work, to create a mark in a downward direction, whereas distortion (overextending and compressing letterforms) is used to reinforce the concept.

ST. PAT'S MASSACRE

Designer: Mark Raebel
Studio: Arsenal Design

Associative Color Response:
• high-chroma green: Saint Patrick's Day

Color Scheme: one hue

In the Saint Patrick's Massacre logomark, symbolism is used (the sword and pierced clover) to communicate the concept. Icon, symbol, and index are excellent tools for designers to help generate an image bank of reference material for any job.

HUGS/REVITAL

Studio: Essex Two

Associative Color Response:
• black: winter

Color Scheme: one hue

Thickness of line is critical when constructing logomarks such as this. Too thin and the mark will fall apart when used at small sizes; too thick and the mark will look clumsy at any size. A logomark or logotype is as good as its weakest link, and in this case the line work will be the first to disappear at a distance.

Test the mark to determine the smallest size it can be used without loss of line work. If the mark holds up at half an inch, it is good.

EUROPE

Designer: Art Chantry

Associative Color Response:
• black: cold, classic

Color Scheme: one hue

Having an excellent type library can lead to unique and appropriate content. Spending time at a university library or national archive may be out of fashion, but it is the most productive way of discovering forgotten typefaces. With today's technology, fonts that are not in current print can be rejuvenated through software applications such as Macromedia's Fontographer, or created into vector art.

LOOSENUT FILMS

Designer: Art Chantry

Associative Color Response:
• black: heavy, solid

Color Scheme: one hue with shades of gray

The gray hues in this logo are accomplished through a continuous-tone line screen. Only one ink is laid down on press, and gray is achieved through tinting (line screen). An ironic metaphoric mark is created through the formal execution of binary opposition.

FOLKLIFE FESTIVAL

Designer: Art Chantry

Associative Color Response:
• black: noble

Color Scheme: one hue

The Folklife Festival logotype is very kinetic. This is achieved by placing the logotype on an upward angle, using an italic typeface, and using a drop shadow to create a 3D illusion on a 2D plane. These three techniques add up to create a wonderfully executed mark.

TEGA

Designer: Tanya A. Ortega
Art Director: John T. Drew

Associative Color Response:
• blue-green: pristine, pure

Color scheme: one hue

The Tega logotype is an experimental design for a fly-fishing outfitting company. The loop of the "g" is extended horizontally to emulate a floating fly-fishing line, and a geometric shape is used to attach and compress the spatial arrangements within the latter half of the mark. This effective technique solidifies numerous letterforms into a cohesive whole.

MAMBOMANIA

Designer: Art Chantry

Associative Color Response:
• black: magical

Color scheme: one hue

The mambo, which Perez Prado originated in the late 1940s, is a Cuban dance similar to the rumba. Two halves—a forward and a backward step—define the basic pattern of the dance. The Mambomania logotype loosely reflects these steps, with the up and down balls indicating the rhythm of the dance. The cross bar of each capital letterform "A" is extended horizontally to indicate the side movement of a mambo dancer's hips. This retro logotype is truly kinetic.

SNOOZE

Designer: Savio Alphonso
Art Director: Theron Moore

Associative Color Response:
• black: spatial, mysterious

Color Scheme: one hue

The logotype consists of grouped circles that form the letters of the word Snooze. This makes the mark intriguing because the viewer has to decipher not only the form of the letters, but also the form of the word.

SAVANNAH HILL

Designers: Kristin Sommese
and Lanny Sommese
Studio: Sommese Design

Associative Color Response:
• mid-range pink-red: soft, subdued, quiet

Color Scheme: one hue with shading

This elegant logomark is beautifully executed through the use of a reductive illustration reinforced with texture. In most cases, quality marks are reduced to the essential elements needed to communicate. An overly complicated mark leads to ambiguity, confusion, and an overall lack of interest. There are exceptions to this rule, however. In this case, the mark is beautifully reduced to the essential elements to create a superior mark.

Savannah Hill

CO ARCHITECTS

Studio: AdamsMorioka

Associative Color Response:
• high-chroma blue: dignity, mature

Color Scheme: one hue

Varying the weight distribution within this logotype places emphasis on "Co" over "Architects"—an excellent technique to emulate the inflections found within speech patterns. The use of capital letterforms gives the appearance of a stable environment. This, coupled with the choice of color, reinforces the idea of a dignified and mature business.

WF

Designer: Shiho Mizuno
Art Director: John T. Drew

Associative Color Response:
• dark green: mature growth, nature

Color Scheme: one hue

Economy of line coupled with gestalt (i.e., the whole is greater than its parts) often creates a mark that has intrigue and interest. Analyzing the structure of the letterforms creating the logotype yields insight into how individual parts can be manipulated and/or eliminated to create intrigue. This allows the audience to engage with the mark through their imagination and fill in the rest of the story.

pure**burn**

ROXIO: PURE BURN

Designer: Stefan G. Bucher
Studio: 344

Associative Color Response:
• black: dark, death, powerful

Color Scheme: one hue

This simple logomark is well executed through the duplication and multiple perspectives. A formal technique celebrated by Cubist artists, and popularized by the likes of Picasso, multiple perspectives add intrigue and individualism to a mark.

SERIOUS ROBOTS

Designer/Art Director: Scott Pridgen

Associative Color Response:
• mid-green: forces, military

Color Scheme: one hue

Choosing the right color for a logomark or logotype is as important as the shape or typefaces used. This logotype is divided into two parts, opposing stillness with motion. This duality creates a kinetic mark by juxtaposing an object that is static with one that appears to be moving. Motion is achieved by the choice of font and the italic cut of this font.

ENOVATION COMPUTERS

Designer: Pelying Li
Art Director: John T. Drew

Associative Color Response:
• high-chroma blue: lively, energetic

Color Scheme: one hue

A 3D illusion on a 2D plane is always a good starting point when creating a mark. The 3D illusion opens up the active white space exponentially, fooling the eye into believing that it can not only move from side to side but also move in, out, through, and around an object. A 3D illusion works best when juxtaposed with a 2D object (flat)—in this example, the name of the company.

KOWALGO HOLDING CO.

Designer: Art Chantry

Associative Color Response:
• black: powerful

Color Scheme: one hue

The boldness of this mark coupled with a sans-serif letterform makes a logo that can be used at any size. This mark could be reduced down to the size of a pencil eraser or smaller and still stay visually intact. This is achieved by an acute awareness of the form/counterform relationships found within the mark.

MOE

Designer: Art Chantry

Associative Color Response:
• black: life, basic

Color Scheme: one hue

The hand-rendered letterforms of the Moe logotype embody uniqueness unsurpassed by any type-foundry font. The kinetic energy achieved through hand rendering is superb; this is an excellent technique to create variation and stylistic differences.

GLEN MOORE

Designer: Art Chantry

Associative Color Response:
• black: spatial, percussion

Color Scheme: one hue

Creating a logotype by hand (i.e., off the computer), is as important today as it has ever been. The uniqueness of form often cannot be achieved through a filter or set action found within contemporary graphic design applications. Constant experimentation with the physicality of form, both on and off the computer, is the only way to master it.

MEET MARKET

Designer/Art Director: Scott Pridgen

Associative Color Response:
• high-chroma red: intense, aggressive

Color Scheme: one hue

The Meet Market logomark uses texture in a highly interesting way. Texture is used both as an indexical reference and as a visual magnet to draw attention to itself. The color red is also used in an indexical manner, to indicate a butcher's seal and to reference red meat.

EARTHED

Designer: Ivan Betancourt
Art Director: John T. Drew

Associative Color Response:
• orange: growing, tasty

Color Scheme: one hue

The meaning of this mark seems to precisely mirror the Associative Color Responses for orange. The metaphorical substitution of a leaf for the "e" further demonstrates the produce qualities associated with this mark.

VIA 101

Studio: AdamsMorioka

Associative Color Response:
• black: powerful, heavy

Color Scheme: one hue

The Via 101 logotype is a simplistic mark that is anatomically conceived so that the logo can be used at any size. This true monoweight typeface is an excellent specimen for viewing at a distance. The letterforms and line weight are exactly the same thickness, creating only one visual angle. If a typeface that has thick and thin relationships is used, multiple visual angles will be created; this means that different parts of the typographic anatomy will disappear at different distances.

CANESTARO

Designer: Javier Cortes

Associative Color Response:
• red: classic, invulnerable

Color Scheme: one hue

The classically formal relationships and symbolism used within this mark communicate longevity. In some cases, it is best to have a logomark that is purposely designed to look as though it has been around for decades. In this context, age equates to the quality of the food and the profitability of the business.

BURMA

Designer: Art Chantry

Associative Color Response:
• black: cold, classic

Color Scheme: one hue

A unique logotype can be created by hand manipulation, by vector manipulation, or by using an unusual font—and this is the case with the Burma mark. The extension of many of the anatomical parts found within the logotype creates an unusual composition—meant to resemble the Myanmar (Burmese) script—that is eloquently defined.

UNION

Designer: Mark Raebel
Studio: Arsenal Design

Associative Color Response:
• black: magical

Color Scheme: one hue

This intriguing logomark uses repetition to represent the idea of union. The circle/ball, located in the center of the mark, has two reflection points that have two ovals rotating around it. This is enclosed by a white square surrounded by a black one. Typographically, the word "union" is repeated twice horizontally and twice vertically. Repetition coupled with pattern or sequence is an excellent technique for uniting and solidifying marks.

TERRAVIDA COFFEE

Studio: Hornall Anderson Design Works

Associative Color Response:
• black: basic

Color Scheme: one hue with tinting (created by a textural halftone screen)

The TerraVida Coffee logotype uses substitution and texture. Substitution is used within the "A" and "V" of TerraVida (coffee leaves). The scale of substitution is subdued in comparison with many of the other marks found within this book. The texture symbolizes the caffeine "buzz" associated with drinking coffee, and resembles the burlap sacks used to ship coffee beans.

TERRAVIDA COFFEE

ORIVO

Studio: Hornall Anderson Design Works

Associative Color Response:
• rust brown: powerful, heavy, strong

Color Scheme: one hue

A weight change within a logotype can create an excellent focal point, engender movement, and demonstrate how a company's name should be pronounced.

ORIVO

SOMMESE DESIGN

Designers/Art Directors: Kristin Sommese and Lanny Sommese
Studio: Sommese Design

Associative Color Response:
• high-chroma red: stimulating

Color Scheme: one hue

The Sommese Design mark was created to represent the two partners of this design firm—a husband-and-wife partnership. The logomark represents the concept of putting two heads together to produce shocking results. The color red was used to reinforce this idea.

YUJIN ONO

Designer: Yujin Ono
Art Director: John T. Drew

Associative Color Response:
• dark green: mature growth

Color Scheme: one hue

Repetition of form is an excellent way to create a logomark. In the Ono mark, one basic shape is repeated to form Yujin's last name. This gives continuity and consistency to the structure of the mark, which is reinforced by the use of one color.

YUJIN ONO

Designer: Yujin Ono
Art Director: John T. Drew

Associative Color Response:
• dark blue: security, service

Color Scheme: one hue

Reducing a logomark to its essential elements is an effective technique for creating quality marks. In most cases, a highly reductive mark will engage the viewer by virtue of gestalt, suggestion, and the viewer's imagination. In this case, the human form is highly active, communicated through four simple shapes. The line work has a severe thick-and-thin relationship to help create a 3D illusion on a 2D plane—this adds to the perceived activity.

WATTS

Designer: Art Chantry

Associative Color Response:
• black: basic, strong

Color Scheme: one hue

In this unusual logotype, distressing is created through the use of repetition; the forms lose their integrity of shape as they are repeated. Kinetic energy is achieved by placing the repeated forms at different intervals; this erratic movement amplifies the grittiness of the mark.

WESTERN COFFEE SHOP

Designer: Art Chantry

Associative Color Response:
• black: distant

Color Scheme: one hue

The Western Coffee Shop logotype is an excellent example of a 3D mark. This is carried out through repetition of form and two-point perspective. The 3D illusion is amplified by juxtaposing "Western" (3D) against "Coffee Shop" (flat).

OKTOBERFEST

Designer: Art Chantry

Associative Color Response:
• black: powerful, heavy

Color Scheme: one hue

The Oktoberfest logomark uses an interesting visual hierarchy. The three figures within the mark are monoweight, bold graphics, and are meant to be seen first. The typography found in the mark is a tertiary element that at a distance, or when used at smaller sizes (less than 1 inch), will collapse on itself, becoming unreadable. This is caused by the small number of counterforms found within the selected font.

PENN STATE JAZZ CLUB

Designer: Kristin Sommese
Art Director/Illustrator: Lanny Sommese
Studio: Sommese Design

Associative Color Response:
• black: mysterious, magical

Color Scheme: one hue

This playful logomark is a superb example of the interplay between form and counterform. By using simile-substitution, a lively and energetic mark that symbolizes the freedom of jazz is created.

7 YEAR BITCH

Designer: Art Chantry

Associative Color Response:
• black: expensive

Color Scheme: one hue

This Art Chantry mark parodies the expression "seven-year itch." This humorous mark is unusual because of the number of signifiers used to communicate the concept (seven). Substitution is used (flames in place of hair) to communicate desire; an empty martini glass to signify being impaired; a young naked woman to communicate both desire and past youth; a ribbon to communicate a trophy; "7-year bitch" to signify being married; and the swirling line work and bubbles to communicate being drunk. This number of signifiers is extremely hard to control, but Art Chantry has done a masterful job.

PITCH AND GROOVE REKORD COMPANY

Designer: Art Chantry

Associative Color Response:
• black: mysterious, heavy

Color Scheme: one hue

Using multiple perspectives is an interesting formal technique to create intrigue within 3D logomarks. In the Punch and Groove logomark, these perspectives juxtaposed with one another create an unorthodox coexistence.

GARTAL

Designer/Art Director: Saied Farisi

Associative Color Response:
• dark red: rich, elegant

Color Scheme: one hue

This interesting logomark is an excellent example of a harmonious relationship between the mark and typeface chosen. When creating a congruous relationship between two elements, harmony is achieved through formal likeness. Note the thick-and-thin relationships, sharpness, and crispness of line, similarity of arcs, and repetition of form.

TOUGH STUFF

Designer: Art Chantry

Associative Color Response:
• black: powerful, strong

Color Scheme: one hue

In the Tough Stuff mark, simile is used within the letterforms of "Stuff" to communicate the meaning of the mark. If all the letterforms had been knocked off the pre-existing horizontal plane, the mark would not be a simile, nor would it communicate the meaning. Opposition is used to create the simile; radically placed type—"STU" is juxtaposed with stationary type—"FF."

BÚHO

Designer: Carlo Irgoyen
Art Director: John T. Drew

Associative Color Response:
• black: powerful, elegant

Color Scheme: one hue

In the Búho logomark, Carlo Irgoyen uses sequential repetition of form to create a simplistically beautiful mark. Repetition of form creates visual consistency.

ONE LOUDER RECORDS

Designer: Art Chantry

Associative Color Response:
• black: invulnerable

Color Scheme: one hue

It is easy to jump on the computer to generate a design solution. However, uniqueness of form is most often carried out by hand. Understanding the physicality of form and how to generate it in many diverse media will enrich the ultimate solution.

MODULAR SYSTEM LOGO

Designer: Songlin Wu
Art Director: John T. Drew

Associative Color Response:
• black: strong, invulnerable

Color Scheme: one hue

This modular system mark creates consistent kinetic energy by repeating and rotating the wedge shape clockwise three times.

ENT

Designer: Francisco Ortiz
Art Director: John T. Drew

Associative Color Response:
• black: expensive

Color Scheme: one hue

When creating logotypes such as the Ent mark, the line width, when reduced to its smallest size, should not exceed .25pt for sheet-fed offset printing, and .33pt for web-fed offset printing. Dropout may occur if the line work is thinner than these specifications. For commercial silkscreen printing, the line weight should be set no thinner than .5pt.

ESTRUS RECORDS

Designer: Art Chantry

Associative Color Response:
• black: strong, powerful

Color Scheme: one hue

The typographic manipulation of this logo is a metaphor to depict the meaning of estrus (being sexually excited and the ability to conceive). This is brought about through the expanded capital letterform "E" and the upward angle of the mark. The outlined letterform "E" operates both as male and female.

ESTRUS RECORDS

Designer: Art Chantry

Associative Color Response:
• black: basic, cold, classic

Color Scheme: one hue

In the E-snail logomark, xerography is used to create the distressed quality of line. This method of working was commonplace prior to the computer age, and is making a comeback today. In fact, any type of texture that can be created off the computer and then scanned in is an excellent method for distressing objects. The problem with most software filters is that they look unnatural; they tend to say "I was done on the computer" and therefore override content.

ESTRUS RECORDS

Designer: Art Chantry

Associative Color Response:
• black: night, life

Color Scheme: one hue

As shown in the Estrus Records logomark, the thickness of line work is excellent for presenting the mark at smaller sizes. When creating a mark that has line work, test the mark by printing the logo as small as it will go. If the line work falls apart prior to the mark being half an inch, the thickness of line will need to be increased.

ESTRUS RECORDS

Designer: Art Chantry

Associative Color Response:
• black: heavy

Color Scheme: one hue

Creating harmony through a perceived action creates unity of form. Note how the person is leaning on the six round balls, pushing the letterforms to become italic.

NON

Designer: Carlo Irgoyen
Art Director: John T. Drew

Associative Color Response:
• high-chroma blue: dignity, pleasing

Color Scheme: one hue

This classically constructed logotype
is pleasing to the eye and uses economy
of line to construct the mark. Both the left
and right stroke of the capital letterform "O" is
also used for the right and left hairline stroke
of the capital letterform "N" on either side of
the "O." If done correctly, this kind of logotype
engages the reader by asking them to use
their imagination.

THE CAPITOL CLUB

Designer: Art Chantry

Associative Color Response:
• black: strong

Color Scheme: one hue

This logomark uses condensed letterforms
to reinforce the idea, through simile (vertical
columns), of the word "capitol." While this
substitution is quite abstract, but aids in
the construction of the mark. When using
substitution, the scale in which it can be used
and the level of abstraction (on a scale from
obvious to obscure) make up the inflections
found within each individual mark.

HOOT NITE

Designer: Art Chantry

Associative Color Response:
• black: noble, night

Color Scheme: one hue

This mark demonstrates how a reductive
illustration can be used to create logos. The
way in which the mouth is illustrated, and the
placement of the box for "hoot night," helps
to convey its humorous demeanor.

REZ

Designer: Savio Alphonso

Associative Color Response:
• black: heavy, basic

Color Scheme: one hue

The Rez logotype is a visual metaphor of its
meaning—a denotative mark that is superbly
executed. Looking up the definition of a word
that directly or indirectly relates to the subject
is an excellent method for conceptual
direction. Many words found within the
dictionary have seven or eight definitions,
each of which can act as a conceptual primer
to foster a visual outcome.

CHUCKIE-BOY RECORDS

Designer: Art Chantry

Associative Color Response:
• black: mysterious

Color Scheme: one hue

This logomark was designed for Chuckie-Boy Records, an alternative record company based in Seattle, Washington. In most cases, creating an anatomically correct illustration yields boring results. The basic inflection of any illustration is brought to bear through the push and pull of line work.

DECK

Designer: Brendan Cosgrove
Art Director: John T. Drew

Associative Color Response:
• dark blue: authoritative, credible

Color Scheme: one hue

The logotype Deck, designed by Brendan Cosgrove, is an excellent example of gestalt. This is a highly effective technique for engaging the audience—viewers must use their imagination to fill in the rest of the information.

RHUBÄRB PHARMACEUTICALS

Designer: Tarun Deep Girdher

Associative Color Response:
• high-chroma blue: strength, sober

Color Scheme: one hue

This dignified logomark creates a pleasing, mature, and provoking statement. Sobering in its execution, the stair-step arrangement creates a counterbalance relationship activating the visual hierarchy.

CITY DELI

Designer/Art Director/Illustrator:
Lanny Sommese
Studio: Sommese Design

Associative Color Response:
• black: elegant

Color Scheme: one hue

The line work found within this mark, coupled with the choice of color, creates a beautiful and elegant mark that is cohesive and visually consistent. Skewing the mark activates the kinetic energy upward.

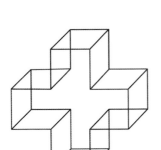

MASS

Designer: Carlo Irgoyen
Art Director: Theron Moore

Associative Color Response:
• high-chroma blue: strength, sober

Color Scheme: one hue

The choice of typeface is outstanding to fit the content and meaning of the logotype. A typographic portrait of "Mass," this mark is beautifully conceived.

GATEWAY MEDICAL

Designer/Illustrator/Art Director:
Lanny Sommese
Studio: Sommese Design

Associative Color Response:
• black: elegant, prestigious

Color Scheme: one hue

This masterfully executed mark incorporates a wonderful 3D illusion. When creating an outlined mark, logomark, or logotype, it is important to consider the line width.

The minimum line width is .25pt for sheet-fed lithography, .33pt for web-fed lithography, and .5pt for commercial silkscreen printing.

BLACK PANTHER

Designer/Illustrator: Lanny Sommese
Art Director: Kristin Sommese
Studio: Sommese Design

Associative Color Response:
• black: spatial, prestigious

Color Scheme: one hue

In general, creating illustrative logomarks that have kinetic energy requires that the illustration not be photorealistic. As seen here, creating a mark that is lively and energetic requires exaggeration of form.

UNIT G DESIGN

Designer: Tanya A. Ortega

Associative Color Response:
• black: heavy

Color Scheme: one hue

This wonderful logotype is an excellent example of joining two dissimilar letterforms into a cohesive whole. This is solidified by the interplay between the loop of the lowercase "g" and the stroke of the lowercase "u"—the loop of the "g" looks as though it is wrapping its leg around the upper ankle of the "u."

I-COPACK

Designer: Linda Liejard

Associative Color Response:
• dark blue: devotion, credible

Color Scheme: one hue

The i-Copack logomark is an excellent example of a reductive mark. The qualitative measure of a mark is directly related to the designer. Understanding the skill sets one possesses is critical in matching the stylistic treatment needed to produce quality.

BSK T BIG BASH

Designer: Art Chantry

Associative Color Response:
• black: heavy

Color Scheme: one hue

This psychedelic logotype is, at its core, a modular system. Twelve rectangular shapes with rounded corners are used to construct the basic mark. A "," mark is used to create the counterforms within each rectangular shape. By doing so, letterforms are created that give the mark its psychedelic look. By building a logotype in this manner, visual consistency is assured—the key component to the success of this mark.

BOSSA:NOVA

Designer: Stefan G. Bucher
Studio: 334

Associative Color Response:
• black: basic

Color Scheme: one hue

The bossa:nova logomark is a superb example of harmonizing the typeface chosen with the mark created. Note how all anatomical parts within the mark have a curvilinear basis and how this relates to the structure of the typeface, including the width to spatial arrangements.

THE HOLIDAYS: SEATTLE

Designer: Art Chantry

Associative Color Response:
• black: powerful

Color Scheme: one hue

In this example, the typeface chosen harmonizes superbly with the illustrative mark. Note how the ears and left side of the cat have the same basic wedge shapes as the forms and counterforms found within the font.

THE MORTALS

Designer: Art Chantry

Associative Color Response:
• black: basic, heavy, powerful

Color Scheme: one hue

Harmonizing the typeface with the mark helps to create a cohesive logo that will stand the test of time. No matter how crudely the image is drawn, if the underpinning structure is sound the quality of the mark will be apparent to the viewer.

SZECHWAN

Studio: modern8

Associative Color Response:
• red: heavy, strong

Color Scheme: one hue

Texture plays an important role in understanding and navigating our environment. No matter how slight, texture acts as a visual magnet.

THUNK

Designer: Art Chantry

Associative Color Response:
• black: basic

Color Scheme: one hue

Repetition of form coupled with texture and off-registration creates a wonderfully kinetic mark. Note how the outline surrounding the mark is incomplete (degraded and disfigured), allowing the eye to pass freely in and out of the mark—this adds to the kinetic energy.

ACE CHAIN LINK FENCE

Studio: Essex Two

Associative Color Response:
• black: strong

Color Scheme: one hue

In the A logotype, the underpinning structure of the mark is symmetrical, making the interlocking forms the focal point. If the line work that created the "A" were asymmetrical, the emphasis and hierarchy would change, thereby diminishing the importance of the interlocking shape.

HOMO HABILIS RECORDS

Designer: Art Chantry

Associative Color Response:
• black: school

Color Scheme: one hue

Adding line work often helps to create kinetic energy to a mark.

ARLINGTON INTERNATIONAL FESTIVAL OF RACING

Studio: Essex Two

Associative Color Response:
• black: prestigious

Color Scheme: one hue

Gestalt is one of the most effective techniques for logo design.

THE WHO

Studio: Essex Two

Associative Color Response:
• black: basic, powerful

Color Scheme: one hue

The Who logotype is an outstanding example of hand-rendered typography. Hand-rendered typography can create a unique form, resulting in a mark of merit.

SLOWBOY

Designer: Art Chantry

Associative Color Response:
• black: magical

Color Scheme: one hue

This wonderfully humorous logomark is anatomically organized. The shape of the boy's head is a vertical structure that harmonizes with the condensed letterforms. The overlapping of image and type just behind the ears makes them stand out, and adds to the lighthearted nature of this mark.

447

Studio: Essex Two

Associative Color Response:
• black: heavy, strong

Color Scheme: one hue

The form/counterform relationship, coupled with the gestalt aspects within this logotype, is quite amazing. Placement of form plays an important role in understanding the spatial arrangement so that gestalt can take place effectively.

JESSICA L. HOWARD

Designer: Jessica L. Howard
Art Director: John T. Drew

Associative Color Response:
• high-chroma blue: lively, pleasing

Color Scheme: one hue

In this asymmetrical logomark, note how the line work seems fluent and natural. This is achieved by devising a measuring stick (a nonstandardized ruler) made from the most common spatial arrangement found within the original mark. This unit of measurement is then subdivided to create a unique ruler to examine and adjust the spatial arrangements. If used correctly, this ruler ensures quality of form/counterform relationships.

CRAFTED WITH PRIDE IN U.S.A.

Studio: Essex Two

Associative Color Response:
• black: basic, elegant

Color Scheme: one hue

In almost every case, creating a modular system to generate a mark will yield a corporate look. The mark (star) is created by using three lines of the same thickness. The three lines are shortened by the same degree, and then rotated to form the star. The more consistency applied within the underpinning structure, the cleaner the mark will look.

PROCTER & GAMBLE: SPANISH

Studio: Essex Two

Associative Color Response:
• black: basic, powerful, heavy

Color Scheme: one hue

In the square sun logomark, repetition of line coupled with scale is used to create agitation within the mark, imparting visual interest.

URBAN SHOPPING CENTER

Studio: Essex Two

Associative Color Response:
• black: basic, invulnerable

Color Scheme: one hue

Substitution is a tried and true technique for developing effective logomarks, and this case is no exception. Note how the simile of form helps to create a cohesive mark.

FIRST HEALTH

Studio: Essex Two

Associative Color Response:
• black: heavy, expensive

Color Scheme: one hue

When using a commonly recognized symbol, it is best to execute it in a unique way so that the mark does not look trite. In this case, the bottom-right part of the heart is shifted to create a tangent point. This allows the eye to move in and out of the mark, creating interest.

TAD

Designer: Art Chantry

Associative Color Response:
• black: powerful, basic, heavy

Color Scheme: one hue

This logotype, created through the process of xerography, is an excellent example of texture creating visual interest. To create a line quality that is degraded, adjust the toner setting and dramatically scale the image up and down when copying.

KLEINPETER

Designer: John R. Kleinpeter
Art Director: John T. Drew

Associative Color Response:
• black: strong, invulnerable

Color Scheme: one hue

This modular-system logomark is achieved using a single shape. The shape is flipped and spaced apart using the same form, creating an energetic and consistent mark.

ENGEMAN'S DREAM WORKS

Designer: Tom Engeman

Associative Color Response:
• black: powerful, basic, heavy

Color Scheme: one hue

Anytime a continuous-tone image is used within the logomark, a coarse halftone screen is advised. The Dreamworks logomark is an excellent example.

ARCH

Designer: Justin Deister

Associative Color Response:
• high-chroma red-orange: youthful, exhilaration

Color Scheme: one hue

The oppositional duality presented in this mark creates an interesting juxtaposition. This complex concept is compressed into two images that are arranged by a distorted use of scale. The building is small and the flame is large—a clever use of opposition.

KRISTIN

Designer: Irene Marx

Associative Color Response:
• dark orange: exhilarating, inspiring, provoking

Color Scheme: one hue

This asymmetrical mark is an excellent example of positioning the focal points, in a triadic relationship, so that the eye is drawn completely through the mark. The hand and feet act as focal points, each performing as one of the three corners within the triad.

HANYANG UNIVERSITY DESIGN GALLERY

Designer: Inyoung Choi

Associative Color Response:
• high-chroma orange: dignity, dramatic

Color Scheme: one hue

The University Design Gallery logotype uses pictograms combined with geometric shapes to communicate the content of the subject matter. The high-chroma blue reinforces the prestige of the gallery.

CENTRAAL MUSEUM: WERELDWIJD WORLDWIDE

Studio: Thonik

Associative Color Response:
• high-chroma red: energetic, cheery

Color Scheme: one hue

The Centraal Museum logotype/mark is created through a modular system, the letterform "c." Stepping and repeating the letterforms achieve visual consistency within the mark. A reductive human figure is created by adapting the logotype into the mark. Note that the line work that makes up the arms, legs, and torso are visually consistent with the stroke width of the letterform "c."

CMP

Studio: BBK Studio

Associative Color Response:
• orange: cheerful
• blue: pure
• green: fresh

Color Scheme: one hue

In the CMP logomark, a contrast in line thickness (thick to thin) is used to create visual intrigue.

NIJNTJE

Studio: Thonik

Associative Color Response:
• high-chroma orange: cheerfulness, energizing

Color Scheme: one hue

This simplistic yet exciting logomark couples clear line work with great execution of form.

POTTYMOUTH

Studio: 86 The Onions

Associative Color Response:
• black: spiritual, basic

Color Scheme: one hue

If done correctly, texture is one of the most effective techniques to create interest. The Pottymouth logo uses three types of texture to create an interesting interplay between the mark and the typeface chosen.

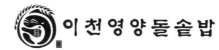

CHO-ICHON RESTAURANT

Designer: Inyoung Choi

Associative Color Response:
• dark red: rich, elegant, refined

Color Scheme: one hue

The dark red (burgundy) hue chosen for this mark is reminiscent of hot wax, and is an excellent choice—the mark is designed as though it is a royal seal.

이천영양돌솥밥

FAT ROOSTER

Designer: Brenda Cox
Art Director: John T. Drew

Associative Color Response:

- high-chroma orange: producing, healing, tasty, growing, fire, warm, cleanliness, happy, cheerfulness, childlike, sunrise, harvest, friendly, loud, pride, wholehearted
- dark blue: serene, quiet, authoritative, credible, devotion, security, service, classic, conservative, strong, dependable, traditional, informed, professional
- high-chroma red: brilliant, intense, energizing, sexy, dramatic, stimulating, active, cheer, joy, fun, aggressive, hope, powerful, warm, overflowing, compassion, heat, hot, fire

Color Scheme: one hue

Color plays an invaluable role in the meaning, interpretation, and physicality of form. Through the use of different hues a mark can be reinterpreted for specific needs. Color has a direct bearing on the distance at which an object can be seen. The dark-blue hue is more visible at a distance than the red and orange hues. In fact, the dark blue is 20% more visible than the orange hue in average daylight. (Dark blue: 79.63; high-chroma red 75.72; high-chroma orange 57.71; these numbers are calculated from white, white being 100.) This may not seem that great a difference. However, as the viewing distance increases so does the viewing gap between hues. For example, at 100 yards an object can be seen in the dark-blue hue, and if the object was the same size in all respects other than its hue (orange) the object would only be seen from a distance of up to 80 yards.

APS CORPORATION

APS CORPORATION

Designer: Linda Liejard

Associative Color Response:

- dark green: mature growth

Color Scheme: one hue

The APS logomark is a wonderful example of a 3D mark using a modular system. The two-point perspective is flawlessly executed, making the illusion believable.

ZANGO

Studio: Hornall Anderson Design Works

Associative Color Response:

- high-chroma orange: energizing

Color Scheme: one hue

In the Zango logotype, the loop of the "g" is manipulated to imply a springlike action. This mark is incredible, especially when applied to colorful, high-chroma collateral materials. The upbeat, high-chroma-orange hue is an excellent choice to reinforce the liveliness of the mark.

WILDLIFE CENTER OF SILICON VALLEY

Designer: Erika Kim

Associative Color Response:
• high-chroma green: life, wilderness, outdoorsy

Color Scheme: one hue

Inspired by the yin and yang symbol, this interwoven logomark is beautifully executed. Taking advantage of the white space found within the mark, substitution was applied to enrich content. The high-chroma green is an excellent color choice for the content (an animal rescue center).

QUIRK

Designer: John Malinoski

Associative Color Response:
• high-chroma yellow: youthful, exhilaration

Color Scheme: one hue

This simile-based mark is an outstanding example of manipulating typography to suit content.

ISLAND SPORTS

Designer: Mark Raebel
Studio: Arsenal Design

Associative Color Response:
• black: basic, magical

Color Scheme: one hue

A mascot or figurine is often an appropriate solution. In this case, the figurine has a retro feel, implying that the company has been around for decades.

HANYANG MUSIC RESEARCH CENTER

Designer: Inyoung Choi

Associative Color Response:
• black: elegant, noble

Color Scheme: one hue

The mark design for the Hanyang Music Research Center uses repetition, fluidity, and 3D aspects within the line work to create a beautifully executed mark that connects to the subject matter.

CENTER FOR DESIGN

Designer: Inyoung Choi

Associative Color Response:
• high-chroma blue-purple: regal, classic, powerful

Color Scheme: one hue

This modular mark is an excellent example of how to create kinetic energy within a logo. The modular unit is stepped, rotated, and repeated to create a cohesive whole. Each element is designed in a progressive manner to create a thick-to-thin relationship that fosters movement within the eye of the viewer.

HUEVOS RANCHEROS

Designer: Art Chantry

Associative Color Response:
• black: basic, night

Color Scheme: one hue

The neutrality of the black color allows the illustrative quality of this humorous mark to gain prominence.

HANYANG MUSIC RESEARCH CENTER

Designer: Inyoung Choi

Associative Color Response:
• black: elegant, noble

Color Scheme: one hue

In this version of the logo for the Hanyang Music Research Center, substitution is used effectively to capture the spirit of the content.

WASHINGTON STATE ECONOMIC REGION 2

Designer: Art Chantry

Associative Color Response:
• black: basic

Color Scheme: one hue

The Region 2 mark uses a reductive illustration of a pinecone and arrowhead shield to communicate "forest"—an excellent example of using no more than two signifiers to communicate a message.

ESTRUS RECORDS

Designer: Art Chantry

Associative Color Response:
• black: basic

Color Scheme: one hue

The quality of line found in the Estrus mark is superbly executed—the mark can be reduced down to any size, and at the same time creates visual interest.

URBAN OUTFITTERS

Designer: Art Chantry

Associative Color Response:
• black: heavy

Color Scheme: one hue

The interaction of mark and typography creates an energetic logo. In this case, the italic font and the reversed type within the black bar create motion and weight that help to connect the object both formally and conceptually.

NEWSPAPER SECTION LOGO

Designer: Art Chantry

Associative Color Response:
• black: invulnerable, mysterious

Color Scheme: one hue

This logomark is an excellent example of matching the quality of line work to the illustration style and subject matter.

WASHINGTON STATE ECONOMIC REGION 7

Designer: Art Chantry

Associative Color Response:
• black: basic

Color Scheme: one hue

The Region 7 mark also uses a reductive illustration to communicate "forest." This time, the illustration is executed in a retro style to give it the appearance of an older mark.

PLASTIC SOLDIER FACTORY

Studio: Plastic Soldier Factory Pte Ltd
Designer: Audrey Koh

Associative Color Response:
- mid-range pink-red: restrained, toned-down, soft, subdued, quiet, sentimental, sober, tame, domestic
- blue-green: pristine, pure, serious, cleanliness, pensive, tranquillity, lively, mellow, cheerful, clarity, consistent, great strength
- high-chroma orange/high-chroma red: energizing, communication, receptive, pride, dramatic, lively, exciting, bright, stimulating, aggressive
- high-chroma green-yellow: new growth, tart, fruity, acidic

Color Scheme: one hue

This universal identity system is executed through a modular system to ensure consistency of shape and line. Although some of the psychological responses to the hues used may not seem to be appropriate for the subject matter, using high-chroma colors ensures a high level of perceived activity by the reader.

DEAUXBOY PRODUCTIONS

Designer: Mike Paz

Associative Color Response:
- neutral gray: quality, classic, timeless

Color Scheme: one hue

When using a continuous-tone image for logos it is best to limit the amount of contrast within the image. By increasing the contrast and limiting the amount of tonal range, the mark will go through a fax machine faster—a more practical solution.

CUSTOM SHIRT SHOP

Designer: Art Chantry

Associative Color Response:
- black: elegant

Color Scheme: one hue

The Custom Shirt Shop logo uses a retro approach. The figure of the woman is positioned in such a way as to express innocence, to give the mark a fresh and clean appearance.

HOLY COW

Designer: Art Chantry

Associative Color Response:
• black: mysterious

Color Scheme: one hue

The Holy Cow mark, designed by Art Chantry, uses multiple perspectives (the double halo) to create an intriguing design.

BRANDU

Designer: Marnita Smith

Associative Color Response:
• gray: invulnerable, heavy

Color Scheme: one hue

The Brandu logotype uses texture to create visual interest. Note how all the textural elements found within the mark harmonize to help create a cohesive whole.

PHOTO TYPO

Designer: Hiroyuki Matsuishi

Associative Color Response:
• black: elegant

Color Scheme: one hue

The hand-drawn letterforms in the Photo Typo logotype are superbly crafted. Note the thick and thin relationships found within the letterforms, and how accent marks are used within the font—a masterful job.

IR 1

Designer: Alex Prompongsatorn
Art Director: John T. Drew

Associative Color Response:
• pastel blue: refreshing, faithful, dependable

Color Scheme: one hue

To create more kinetic energy, place the mark or letterform off-center. This technique creates a more dynamic, asymmetrical design.

DOT

Designer: Elle Osorio
Art Director: John T. Drew

Associative Color Response:
• black: heavy, strong

Color Scheme: one hue

Type reversals knocked out of solid letter-forms is an excellent technique for creating uniqueness of form. The form/counterform relationship found within this logotype serves to create a visual depiction of meaning (dot).

SUN TZU REPORT

Designer: Chen Wang

Associative Color Response:
• neutral gray/blue-green: timeless, pristine, further

Color Scheme: one hue

This modular mark uses a step, scale-down, and repeat pattern that is copied and inverted.

ESTHER J. KIM

Designer: Esther J. Kim

Associative Color Response:
• violet: elegant

Color Scheme: one hue

The Esther Kim logotype uses hand-drawn letterforms to create the mark—an excellent formal technique to create visual interest.

EGI

Designer: Aurieanne Lopez
Art Director: John T. Drew

Associative Color Response:
• neutral gray/blue-green: pristine, timeless, further

Color Scheme: one hue

Several formal techniques are employed in the egi logotype. Substitution of anatomical parts within the lowercase letterform "g," coupled with gestalt and use of counterforms, creates an intriguing mark. Substitution is carried out through an expanded "~" mark of the same font.

WILLIE WEAR A CONDOM

Designer: Art Chantry

Associative Color Response:
• black: powerful

Color Scheme: one hue

The figurine of a condom coupled with the "blue ribbon" prize creates a humorous juxtaposition of type and image. Note the positioning of the rocket within the blue ribbon.

CALIFORNIA STATE POLYTECHNIC UNIVERSITY

Designer: Deborah Lem
Art Director: Babette Mayer

Associative Color Response:
• black: powerful, elegant

Color Scheme: one hue

This logomark is a composite of two indexical references found on the university campus—a building and orchards. If done correctly, this is an excellent process to create a logomark.

SONIA LUQUE

Designer: Sonia Luque
Art Director: John T. Drew

Associative Color Response:
• pastel blue: refreshing, faithful, happy

Color Scheme: one hue

Using the punctuation marks and symbols found within a font is a good technique for creating unique solutions. Holding down the option key while selecting the numbers and letters on the keyboard will access all punctuation and symbols associated with the font.

NATIONAL ENDOWMENT FOR THE ARTS

Designers: Tom Engeman, Ned Drew, and Richard Crest

Associative Color Response:
• black: powerful, strong

Color Scheme: one hue

The National Endowment for The Arts logomark is a good example of not enclosing the entire shape. By allowing the mark to breathe, activating the white space, the eye can move in and out of the mark. If the mark was enclosed, for example a circle around an object, the white space will not be activated.

NATIONAL ENDOWMENT FOR THE ARTS

KASHOKAI

Designer: Hiroyuki Matsuishi

Associative Color Response:
• dark red: strong, taste, mature

Color Scheme: one hue

The Kashokai logotype is a unique blend of Japanese characters and roman alphabet to spell out the same word. The dark-red hue is an excellent choice of color to represent this company.

PEACE

Designer: Hiroyuki Matsuishi

Associative Color Response:
• high-chroma red: blood, powerful, dangerous

Color Scheme: one hue

Here, an irony-based metaphor is created through substitution—the guns spell out the Japanese character for "peace."

THE PARK

Designer: Kristin Sommese
Illustrator: Lanny Sommese
Art Directors: Kristin Sommese and Lanny Sommese
Studio: Sommese Design

Associative Color Response:
• black: magical, noble

Color Scheme: one hue

This mark for a local conservation group is inviting. It fosters an awareness of the positive impact of urban green space and the precarious nature of an unprotected environment. The bird is intricately linked to the park through consistent stroke weights in both the legs and the type. Protection and caring is implied through the negative and positive hands visible in the counters of the bird's wings.

MONOMEN HERE'S HOW

Designer: Art Chantry

Associative Color Response:
• black: magical, night

Color Scheme: one hue

This humorous and retro logomark is designed with the human figure mooning the moon. Stacked typography is not often used because of readability concerns—it is the most unreadable configuration for roman type. However, in this mark, the vertical type helps the compositional balance and complements the retro feel.

MORPHOSIS ARCHITECTURE INC.

Designer: Sisi Xu
Art Director: John T. Drew

Associative Color Response:
• dull gold: radiant, prestigious

Color Scheme: one hue

The elegance of form and the subtle revelation of each letter in this mark suggest prestige, quality, and achievement. The "a" as a counterform seems to radiate out from the warm background color.

ZUMAYA

Designer: Shannon Ramsay

Associative Color Response:
• black: spatial, percussion

Color Scheme: one hue

This mark moves by flowing thick and thin forms around the central black core. These forms reiterate the circle through the white counterform present in the outline of the circle.

COLLEGE OF EDUCATION AND INTEGRATIVE STUDIES

Designer: Babette Mayor

Associative Color Response:
• black: elegant, strong

Color Scheme: one hue

Continuing on the theme found in the logo of the affiliated California State Polytechnic (see page 39), references to orchards are used for the College of Education and Integrative Studies. The lowercase letterform

"e" is manipulated to create an organic harmonious relationship between the leaf and letterform used.

CATHOLIC CAMPUS MINISTRY

Designer/Art Director: Ned Drew

Associative Color Response:
• high-chroma blue: dignity, service

Color Scheme: one hue

The Catholic Campus Ministry logomark is an excellent example of harmonizing the font with the mark. This is brought about through the consistency of stroke width, not only in the font but in the mark as well. The juxtaposition of the three signifiers (cross, heart, dove) creates a symbol for the campus ministry.

HARBOUR SUITES

Designer/Art Director: Scott Pridgen

Associative Color Response:
• brown: sheltering, warm

Color Scheme: one hue

The calligraphic font helps to convey a rich, warm, and rather lavish environment with an emphasis on traditional hospitality.

The lushness of the brush strokes is counterbalanced by the sans-serif letterforms, giving the audience the feeling that the establishment is both inviting and professional.

TEGA

Designer: Tanya A. Ortega
Art Director: John T. Drew

Associative Color Response:
• high-chroma blue-green: new, fresh

Color Scheme: one hue

The line quality of the mark suggests forward movement. In addition, the elimination of the thin strokes within the letterforms completes the connotation of motion by replicating what happens to type viewed at a distance. The thinnest part of the stroke is hardest to discern at a distance and will greatly diminish legibility.

AQUATICS & EXOTICS PET STORE

Designer/Illustrator/Art Director:
Lanny Sommese
Studio: Sommese Design

Associative Color Response:
• blue-green: pristine, cheerful

Color Scheme: one hue

The ambiguity of the animals illustrated in this mark is in keeping with the variety of species available in an exotic pet store. The blue-green can be related to both water and

vegetative habitats. The purity of the color bolsters the simultaneous contrast and thereby the positive/negative effect.

MEXICAN DOORBELL

Designer: Art Chantry

Associative Color Response:
• black: death, night

Color Scheme: one hue

The Chihuahua has been silenced in this humorous and sardonic mark.

RAHFAR ARCHITECTURE

Designer: Saied Farisi

Associative Color Response:
• purple: elegant, meditative

Color Scheme: one hue

It is important for an architectural firm to represent itself as dependable and trustworthy. Here, the color helps to distinguish the firm

as a thoughtful consultancy interested in creating classic design that is both elegant and forward-thinking.

FARISI

Designer: Saied Farisi

Associative Color Response:
• black: life, mysterious

Color Scheme: one hue

The minimal owl is fanciful and mysterious. The eyes seem to peer into the viewer due to their imbalance of white. This effect is created through simultaneous contrast, which is most pronounced in disproportionate quantities of color.

FARISI

Designer: Saied Farisi

Associative Color Response:
• dark orange: exhilarating, stimulating

Color Scheme: one hue

The fluidity of line and kinetic energy of this logotype are achieved through the thick and thin relationships. This is an excellent hand-rendered technique for creating logomarks or logotypes, and is particularly effective when coupled with an appropriate choice of color.

FARISI

Designer: Saied Farisi

Associative Color Response:
• black: elegant, noble

Color Scheme: one hue

The unequal relationship between the foreground color (black) and the background color (white) within this mark helps to accentuate the eyes. This phenomenon, coupled with thick-to-thin relationships found with the line work, creates a kinetic mark.

FLUX

Designer: Diana Gonzalez
Art Director: Jen Bracy

Associative Color Response:
• black: school, noble

Color Scheme: one hue

This logotype for a nonprofit organization dedicated to educating young people in careers in art and design communicates through form and color by reiterating its mission to promote continual growth and change. The metamorphosis of the font and the strength of the color support the idea that design can change the individual and the world—a noble mission.

ART RESOURCES

Designer: Saied Farisi

Associative Color Response:
• blue: tranquil, devoted to noble ideas

Color Scheme: one hue

This logomark for a handmade rug, sculpture, and handicraft distributor features the classic lines evident in Persian antiquities and a color often associated with the market.

DIANA GONZALEZ

Designer: Diana Gonzalez

Associative Color Response:
• high-chroma red-purple: sophisticated, creative

Color Scheme: one hue

The playful acronym for Diana Gonzalez, graphic designer, is carefully evoked through the subtle slant of the letterforms and shift

in foreground and background through the "d" and "G." This, in combination with a well-defined usage of associative color, implies that the designer has strong conceptual abilities and high energy that will yield thoughtful design.

AR

Designer: Leon Shultz-Ray
Art Director: John T. Drew

Associative Color Response:
• pastel blue: tranquil, dependable

Color Scheme: one hue

Here, the smooth transitions of each letterform reiterate the color's associative responses of calm, tranquillity, and peacefulness, while the italic, serif font choice further defines the acronym as timeless and dependable.

3

FONDS ALEXANDRE ALEXANDRE

Designer/Illustrator/Art Director:
Lanny Sommese
Studio: Sommese Design

Associative Color Response:
• black: spatial, magical

Color Scheme: one hue

The intertwined relationship between film and art is exemplified in this logo for a collection of posters on those subjects. Each is seen as indelibly influencing the other and inseparable in content. This idea creates depth and

dimensionality to the individual's artistic effort defined through the substitution of a brush and film leader for fingers of a hand.

INTER VALLEY SYSTEMS

Designer/Illustrator/Art Director:
Lanny Sommese
Studio: Sommese Design

Associative Color Response:
• green: compassion, empathy

Color Scheme: one hue

Empathy, camaraderie, and a natural compassionate flow of energy is exemplified through the calming green color and the smooth transitions of circular shapes.

PENN STATE JAZZ CLUB

Designer: Kristin Sommese
Illustrator/Art Director: Lanny Sommese
Studio: Sommese Design

Associative Color Response:
• black: magical, percussion

Color Scheme: one hue

The elongated forms and black rectangle create a perceived banner that is reminiscent of a marching-band flag. The whimsical counterforms seem to spill from the instruments with a lyrical quality.

THE UNTAMED YOUTH

Designer: Art Chantry

Associative Color Response:
• black: powerful, mysterious

Color Scheme: one hue

The cropping of the shoulder and head on the left seem to imply a coquettish revealing of the human form. Sardonic humor is expressed through the text written across the body and its disproportionate relationship to the arm.

THE CHILDREN'S CARE CENTER

Designer/Illustrator/Art Director:
Lanny Sommese
Studio: Sommese Design

Associative Color Response:
• purple: charming, tender

Color Scheme: one hue

The Children's Care Center logo is emotive without being juvenile or disrespectful of the work done by childcare providers. The color of the mark creates a tender and sweet quality.

HANDLE WITH CARE

Studio: Essex Two

Associative Color Response:
• black: basic, sober

Color Scheme: one hue

This mark for the US Department of Labor Accident Prevention Program creates a strong, clear, and objective statement that, if handled with care, damage can be avoided. The type and line quality of the form are also heavy and minimal, reinforcing the rather sober message.

FERRIS UNIVERSITY BULL DOGS

Studio: Essex Two

Associative Color Response:
• black: powerful, invulnerable

Color Scheme: one hue

The thick black line around the bulldog mascot creates an impressive and imposing force that is Ferris State University athletics.

The stark contrast, sharp line quality, and edgy collar create a professional and yet slightly youthful mark that appeals to college ages.

FREEDOM HOME CARE

Studio: Essex Two

Associative Color Response:
• high-chroma blue: serenity, dignity

Color Scheme: one hue

The mark for Freedom Home Care, an in-home healthcare organization, epitomizes the healing hands of

a calm, caring professional. Rather than repeating typical health-industry metaphors, this mark emphasizes the service, dignity, and respect that a patient deserves.

MICHAEL STEIN VOICE TALENT

Designer: Art Chantry

Associative Color Response:
• black: magical, mysterious

Color scheme: one hue

This mark is lyrical and humorous, referencing an uncanny ability to change one's voice. The implication is made through the grainy quality of the black ventriloquist's dummy as well as the lighthearted but eerie facial expression.

DANTE'S TAKEOUT

Designer/Illustrator/Art Director:
Lanny Sommese
Studio: Sommese Design

Associative Color Response:
• black: classic, basic

Color Scheme: one hue

The contrasting forms create a quick read that says, "Food can be gotten here." The minimalist approach implies instant gratification through classic cuisine.

FISK

Designer: Art Chantry

Associative Color Response:
• black: basic, bold

Color Scheme: one hue

This utilitarian mark for Fisk harks back to the aerodynamic quality of 1950s design.

LAB USEFUL

Designer: Savio Alphonso

Associative Color Response:
- red: surging, brilliant, intense, energizing, dramatic
- orange: healing, tasty, growing, cheerfulness, warm
- brown: rustic, deep, rich, folksy, rooted, sheltering, durable
- black: classic, basic

Color Scheme: one hue

The knockout of this simple mark distinctly changes associative color meaning with each ink. This red carries an intensity and energy, the brown is stable and secure, while the orange produces a cheerful, gregarious response. These subtle shifts illustrate the power color holds as a message carrier.

RUSH

Designer: Savio Alphonso

Associative Color Response:
- red: excitement, energizing

Color Scheme: one hue

In placing a food product, it is crucial that the customer is aware of the product's benefits and develops loyalty through a maintained brand identity. The marketability of Rush lies in the fact that it is a caffeinated beverage. Therefore, every component of the design reiterates this key content. For example, the pixelated font (Emigre Eight) and the color convey the stimulating and subtly jarring effects of caffeine.

THE X-RAYS

Designer: Art Chantry

Associative Color Response:
- black: powerful, mysterious

Color Scheme: one hue

This is a provocative and powerful image that playfully builds on the concept of "X" meaning "explicit," while simultaneously censoring the frontal pose to further the mystique and pique curiosity. To further the pun, all of the mystery could be hypothetically revealed if the viewer had the fabled X-ray vision illustrated in superhero comics.

Two Colors

One- and two-color logos are still the most
commonly used today. Budgetary constraints
can inspire a multitude of intriguing color palettes,
be it for logomarks, logotypes, or simple symbols,
as these constraints often force designers to consider
alternative, more original, measures in solving a design
problem. Simplifying the color palette can enhance
the design direction by placing limits that facilitate
superior and inspirational marks.

Simplified color palettes can control the look, feel,
dimension, legibility, readability, direction, harmony,
discord, and kinetic energy of a mark. The inherent
energy found within a mark, and applied through
color, is most often intentional. In addition, its color
association and learned behavioral effects and/or
psychological attributes enhance communication
by amplifying the tone, texture, form, silhouette,
and ultimately combine to facilitate the objectives.

ASPPA PAC

Studio: Bremmer & Goris Communications

Associative Color Response:
• red shade: benevolent, compassion
• high-chroma blue: honesty, dignity

Color Scheme: primaries

This series of marks for the ASPPA communicates confidence and forward-thinking. The lean to the right of each white counterform becomes a foreground image that reiterates progress, while the color defines integrity. Some colors, such as the red and blue of the United States flag, communicate strength, solidarity, and dignity. The slight shading of the traditional flag red dampens the virility and increases the trustworthy undertones. The intensification of the traditional flag blue creates a more energetic and proactive composition. These colors, with the white of the Capitol Building, put the committee in context.

ASPPA PENSION EDUCATION AND RESEARCH FOUNDATION

Studio: Bremmer & Goris Communications

Associative Color Response:
• green shade: mature growth
• yellow-orange: healthy

Color Scheme: near incongruent with shade

ASPPA's membership comprises a diverse group of individuals working in the highly regulated private pension industry. The organization offers educational opportunities, credentialing, and legislative tracking and information to its membership. The primary organizational mark seeks to encapsulate the mission and communicate its desire to keep abreast of the changing needs of the retirement plan industry. Both colors show the healthy growth a successful pension fund seeks to attain.

ASPPA MARKETPLACE

Studio: Bremmer & Goris Communications

Associative Color Response:
• dark blue: service
• high-chroma blue: rich

Color Scheme: analogous

As a continuation of the ASPPA series, this Marketplace logo emphasizes service, professionalism, and accessibility through a confident color choice.

2005: YEAR OF THE ROOSTER

Designer: Chen Wang

Associative Color Response:
• high-chroma red: energizing, joy, fun
• black: noble, spiritual, magical

Color Scheme: hue plus neutral

The color combination of red and black helps to create a fun and exciting atmosphere in which all Americans can enjoy and promote Chinese culture—red and black also symbolize traditional Chinese values. The simple flat shapes found within the mark allow for ease of printing. The posters and T-shirts for the festival were silkscreen, adding a richness of color unsurpassed by any other form of printing—in silkscreen printing the inks are more opaque and a greater ink volume can be laid down on press to produce lush colors.

PREVENT FIRE. SAVE LIVES.

Studio: Bremmer & Goris Communications

Associative Color Response:
• high-chroma orange: receptive
• gray: sober

Color Scheme: one hue plus neutral

The color scheme for this mark clearly communicates fire and ash without being blatantly inflammatory—the antithesis of the concept. The orange attracts the eye and requests the audience to soberly accept responsibility for the prevention of fires.

CUTIES ON DUTY

Studio: Bremmer & Goris Communications

Associative Color Response:
• high-chroma pink: fun
• black: neutral

Color Scheme: hue plus neutral

High-chroma pink is an attention-grabbing color that makes the black almost disappear. The vibrant pink exudes excitement and inspires a genial atmosphere.

QATAR PETROLEUM

Designer: Tarek Atrissi

Associative Color Response:
• pastel green: calm, quiet, natural
• high-chroma blue: dignity, mature

Color Scheme: simple analogous

The choice of hues for the Qatar Petroleum logomark is devised to create a public image of a clean and natural product. The use of color as propaganda to communicate the opposite traits of an industry is an interesting approach—it makes people feel good even though they know better.

PALENQUE

Designer: Carlo Irgoyen
Art Director: John T. Drew

Associative Color Response:
• high-chroma red: warm, active
• purple: prestigious, strong

Color Scheme: one hue plus neutral

The Palenque logomark is an excellent example of color choice. This color combination helps to create an exciting and energetic mark that also indicates, when placed in context, the atmosphere and geographical location.

MT

Designer: Anna Marie
Art Director: John T. Drew

Associative Color Response:
• yellow-green: (with shading)
• blue-violet: new growth, regal, classic

Color Scheme: two points of a triadic color palette (tertiary hues)

The color combinations of yellow-green and blue-violet create a classical environment that communicates new growth. The line work in this logotype is exceptionally executed to maximize the use of gestalt.

RPM

Designer: Carlo Irgoyen
Art Director: John T. Drew

Associative Color Response:
• dark orange: exhilarating, inspiring
• dark blue: authoritative, credible

Color Scheme: complementary with shading

The RPM logotype uses a conservative color palette, through the use of shading, that denotes an authoritative tone. The logotype uses gestalt to generate interest by revealing just enough information to understand the mark without making it obvious. In most cases, to make a mark obvious is to create a logo that is trite.

AVREK FINANCIAL CORPORATION

Designer: Carlo Irgoyen
Art Director: John T. Drew

Associative Color Response:
• earth-tone orange: rich, warm, strength
• high-chroma blue: lively, strength, dramatic

Color Scheme: complementary with tinting and shading

Color plays an important role in how a company wants to be viewed by the public, especially when it is dealing with an individual's personal assets. In this case, color sets the tone by making sure the audience views the company in a warm and inviting way, while at the same time making them feel secure.

BCC CUSTOM TILE AND STONE

Designer: Chad Dewilde
Studio: The Beautiful Design

Associative Color Response:
• earth tone: strength, wholesome, rooted
• high-chroma blue: honesty, strength, lively

Color Scheme: near complementary with shading

In a highly competitive market, the BCC Custom Tile and Stone logomark needs to communicate in a more direct manner than its rivals. The color palette helps soften the directness of the mark by implying the values of the company and thereby potentially capturing a greater customer base.

FAT ROOSTER

Designer: Brenda Cox
Art Director: John T. Drew

Associative Color Response:
• high-chroma orange: thought, pride, exciting
• high-chroma blue-purple: powerful

Color Scheme: near complementary

When creating a color palette, it is often best to use a disproportionate amount of one color over another. An accent color tends to draw attention to itself by virtue of oppositional techniques. In this case, the oppositional techniques are small to large, and cool to warm colors—cool colors recede and warm colors advance. These techniques create a high degree of kinetic energy within the Fat Rooster logotype.

INSTITUTE FOR LEARNING & COMMUNITY DEVELOPMENT

Studio: Bremmer & Goris Communications

Associative Color Response:
• high-chroma violet: creative, unique
• high-chroma yellow-green: new growth

Color Scheme: near complementary

The purple shade gives a rich and sophisticated touch to children's playful building blocks. The green increases the depth and helps to rotate the purple forms in an upward progressive direction. In addition, the green tint suggests new growth without appearing childish.

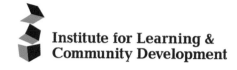

HD

Designer: Maja Bagic
Creative/Art Directors: Davor Bruketa and Nikola Zinic

Associative Color Response:
• high-chroma yellow-green: new growth
• earth-tone red: warm-hearted

Color Scheme: near complementary with shading

Through the use of color, the "hd" logotype is a wonderful example of promoting an environmentally friendly company. It also generates a corporate image that reflects the future growth of the company.

LUBBOCK CHINESE AMERICAN ASSOCIATION

Designer: Chen Wang

Associative Color Response:
• black: powerful, elegant
• dark gray: wise, cultured

Color Scheme: one hue with shading (achromatic)

Designer Chen Wang used a simple achromatic color scheme to help speed recognition of the logotype. The Lubbock Chinese American Association mark uses a gray square to delineate the "L" from the "C"—an outstanding practical application of color.

THE LANGUAGE KEY

Studio: Bremmer & Goris Communications

Associative Color Response:
• high-chroma green-yellow: new growth
• gray: neutral

Color Scheme: hue plus neutral

The addition of black to the green-yellow tones down the acidic qualities and imbues the mark with a sense of new growth tempered by experience. The gray further reiterates the practicality of education in a timeless manner.

FISHING OUTFITTERS

Designer: Edwin Alvarenga
Art Director: John T. Drew

Associative Color Response:
• pastel blue-violet: pleasure, water
• high-chroma blue-violet: classic, regal

Color Scheme: simple monochromatic

This mark, designed for a fishing outfitting company, is an excellent example of using selected hues and a simple color scheme to help convey the psychological effects associated with fishing.

CHOICE ONE MEDICAL

Designer: Doug Herberich

Associative Color Response:
• high-chroma blue: calm, relaxed
• high-chroma blue-violet: classic, tender

Color Scheme: simple analogous

Color has context. Depending upon the industry in which the color is used, different psychological and learned behavioral effects will be associated with the color or colors used. Different environments will change our perception of the same hues and color schemes, both physically and psychologically.

ADRIS

Creative/Art Directors: Davor Bruketa and Nikola Zinic

Associative Color Response:
• black: powerful, strong
• high-chroma blue-violet: classic

Color Scheme: one hue with neutral

The Adris logotype is an excellent example of gestalt. In this case, the crossbar of the capital "A" is removed, making the mark

interesting by engaging the audience's imagination to envision the missing part. Without the removal of the crossbar this mark would be uninteresting—the mark's story would be told in an obvious way.

ALEXANDER CONSTRUCTION

Designer: Chad Dewilde
Studio: The Beautiful Design

Associative Color Response:
• pastel green: complete, natural
• pastel blue-green: pristine, serious

Color Scheme: near simple analogous with tinting

Choosing the right color palette for a company says a lot about the values the company holds dear. In this case, the use of the index images combined with the choice of colors creates the perfect company image.

ABSOLUTE

Designer: Jeff Sandford

Associative Color Response:
• olive: strong
• high-chroma yellow-green: new growth

Color Scheme: one hue with neutral

This robust logotype is a fine example of gestalt, harmony of form, and color choice. Note that the typeface chosen for "Absolute" and the "A" mark above have the same stroke

width, creating harmony of form. The "A" mark is a modified "A" that is not entirely spelled out (the sum is greater than its parts), and the yellow-green and black create a powerful and dynamic color palette.

PLANT ZERO

Designer: John Malinoski

Associative Color Response:
- high-chroma red: brilliant, energizing
- high-chroma red-magenta: warm, healing
- neutral gray: quality, passion
- high-chroma yellow-orange: stimulating, fun
- high-chroma yellow-green: sunlight, new growth

Color Scheme: simple analogous (red); one hue with neutral (gray); primary, secondary, random (yellow-orange); near complementary (yellow-green)

In this color study, the legibility, readability, and behavioral effects can be assessed to determine which mark functions best. When comparing the four studies, Plant Zero 1 should not be used at any distance greater than 18 to 24 inches. The two hues within this color study are a metameric pair—they have the same spectral reflectance curve (CV)

in at least one light source, making it all but impossible to distinguish shape at a distance. In the gray, yellow, and green versions, the red dot can be seen at a greater distance than its counterpart. The yellow logo breaks the 20% rule of thumb, however, the neutral gray is the second-most visible color at a distance. The yellow-orange is the third-most visible and the yellow-green is the least visible. At the mark's maximum distance, the red dot will be seen and nothing else. The neutral gray is roughly 15% more visible, at a distance, than the yellow-orange, and is roughly 20% more visible than the yellow-green. In some cases, colors that have 20% or less CVD cannot be distinguished from one another. This is why the rule exists. However, this is not the case with yellow logo here.

HIDAKA PRINTING

Designer: Hiroyuki Matsuishi

Associative Color Response:
- black: strong
- high-chroma red: intense, energizing

Color Scheme: one hue with neutral

Black and high-chroma red are one of the most successful color combinations ever used. In most cases, this color combination will create a powerfully strong and energetic mark.

HIDAKA PRINTING

CALIFORNIA STATE POLYTECHNIC UNIVERSITY, POMONA, COLLEGE OF BUSINESS

Designer: Babette Mayor

Associative Color Response:
- high-chroma yellow-green: strength
- black: prestigious

Color Scheme: one hue plus neutral

California State Polytechnic University, Pomona (CPP) was first established as an agricultural campus on land endowed by W. K. Kellogg, the cereal entrepreneur and Arabian horse aficionado. In honor of this history and in deference to the university's logomark, the College of Business logomark integrates a green leaf into the counterform of the lowercase "b". The green is a vibrant tint of the university's green, implying new growth, sharp business sense, and unlimited potential. These associated attributes help define the College of Business.

business@csupomona.edu

FOUNTAIN HEAD

Designer: John Malinoski

Associative Color Response:
- high-chroma red: intense, energizing
- high-chroma yellow-green: new growth

Color Scheme: near complementary

The color combination for this whimsical mark is a perfect metaphor for the conceptual statement being made—the psychological and learned behavioral effects of the hues harmonize with the illustration.

TRIDVAJEDAN

Designer/Art Director: Izvorka Serdarevic

Associative Color Response:
- high-chroma blue: rich, upward
- black: powerful, cold, classic

Color Scheme: one hue with neutral

The Tridvajedan logo color scheme is an ideal choice for this corporate logomark. The high-chroma blue juxtaposed with the black letterforms creates a strong, classic, and upward-moving mark.

EXPO DESIGN: PUBLIC PROCUREMENT SERVICE

Designer: Inyoung Choi

Associative Color Response:
- high-chroma blue: rich, upward
- high-chroma blue-violet: powerful, classic, futuristic

Color Scheme: simple analogous

The gradient found within this logomark amplifies the kinetic energy and, at the same time, helps to create a 3D illusion. Using gradients within marks is a delicate matter.

If done poorly, the mark will date quickly and/or look trite; in this case, however, the gradient is handled masterfully.

CAT HEAD

Designer: Art Chantry

Associative Color Response:
- high-chroma red: aggression, excitability
- black: powerful, strong

Color Scheme: one hue with neutral

The color scheme of red and black are well suited for this energetic mark. If you use drop shadows, make sure you use them in a way

that amplifies the content, otherwise this technique looks dated and trite. In the Cat Head mark, the dropped shadow is used masterfully to amplify the kinetic energy found within the letterforms.

ARSENAL DESIGN

Designer: Mark Raebel
Studio: Arsenal Design

Associative Color Response:
- neutral gray: quality, classic, timeless
- high-chroma yellow-orange: enterprise, drive, goal, powerful

Color Scheme: one hue with neutral (tinted)

The color palette in the Arsenal Design logomark is well suited to reflect the qualities associated with this coat of arms or family crest. The high-chroma orange is associated with an enterprising company that strives to create quality.

KELLY'S SEAFOOD SHACK

Designer: Kelly Thacker
Art Director: John T. Drew

Associative Color Response:
- high-chroma blue: water, ice, service
- neutral gray: quality, classic

Color Scheme: one hue with neutral (tinted)

The Kelly's Seafood Snack logomark is an excellent example of an ink rubbing. To create an ink rubbing, use a spray bottle filled with India ink. Using the mist setting, spray down the object, carefully place butcher's paper on top of the object, and rub. In this case, an ink rubbing is appropriate for the content (historically, Japanese fishermen would ink-rub the catch of the day). This formal technique can yield interesting marks.

DEVELOPMENT PARTNER PILOT PROGRAM

Designer/Art Director: Jun Li
Studio: Juno

Associative Color Response:
- black: powerful, strong
- neutral gray: quality, classic

Color Scheme: one hue with neutral (tinted)

The Development Partner Pilot Program logotype is a fine example of a modular system. Constructed from only two shapes (a square and a triangle), this mark reads the same either right-side-up or upside-down. Color is used to delineate between the "D" and "P"—a great example of the practical use of color.

HGC

Designer: Julie J. Park
Art Director: John T. Drew
Studio: Juno

Associative Color Response:
- high-chroma orange: producing, growing, strong
- earth-tone brown: durable

Color Scheme: simple analogous with shading

In this example, the arts of substitution and gestalt are executed to a high level. A ")" is used from the same font by rotating it at 90 degrees and substituting it for the loop of the lowercase "g." Gestalt is used to give the lowercase "g" just enough visual clues to determine what it is.

EXPO DESIGN: NATIONAL INSTITUTE OF KOREAN HISTORY

Designer: Inyoung Choi

Associative Color Response:
- neutral gray: producing, growing, strong
- high-chroma blue: durable

Color Scheme: one hue with neutral (tinted)

Designer Inyoung Choi creates a magnificent 3D illusion on a 2D plane. This is carried out through the use of two-point perspective and color choice.

EXPO DESIGN: MINISTRY OF UNIFICATION

Designer: Inyoung Choi

Associative Color Response:
• high-chroma yellow-green: new growth
• high-chroma blue: mature, upward

Color Scheme: near incongruous

In silkscreen printing, a split fountain is achieved when more than one ink is placed in the fountain—that is, on the screen. Typically, these are spaced apart so that a cascade of different hues is achieved. Here, designer Inyoung Choi creates the equivalent of a split fountain on the computer to achieve a masterfully created gradient of hues.

INTELLIVUE UNPLUGGED

Designer: Jun Li

Associative Color Response:
• high-chroma orange: healing, warm
• high-chroma blue: mature, upward

Color Scheme: direct complementary

A direct complementary color palette is best suited for asymmetrical design such as the IntelliVue Unplugged logomark. This color scheme creates simultaneous contrast when used in butt register and in disproportionate amounts. Kinetic energy is induced anytime opposition occurs. Applying harmony to composition is more suited to symmetrical design. With that said, there is a scale to everything. The more formal techniques used to induce kinetic energy, the more likely the composition is to be asymmetrical, and vice versa.

THE FRISKY BISCUIT BREAD COMPANY

Designer: Mark Raebel
Studio: Arsenal Design

Associative Color Response:
• black: elegant, magical
• high-chroma red-violet: sweet taste

Color Scheme: one hue with neutral

For practical reasons, any time a continuous-tone image is used for part or all of a mark, it is critical to use a gross screen pattern such as The Frisky Biscuit Bread Company logo. The coarser the screen pattern, the faster the logo will go through a fax machine.

EXPLORERS INCORPORATED

Designer: Mark Raebel
Studio: Arsenal Design

Associative Color Response:
• black: powerful, strong
• high-chroma yellow-orange: enterprise, drive, goal, powerful

Color Scheme: one hue with neutral

The choice of hues within the Explorers Incorporated logomark suits the subject matter. Yellow-orange and black create a powerfully strong and enterprising color scheme.

ANEMONE MAKEUP

Designer: Mark Raebel
Studio: Arsenal Design

Associative Color Response:
- neutral gray: quality, classic, timeless
- mid-green: classic

Color Scheme: one hue with neutral (tinted)

The color schemes found in the Anemone Makeup logomark is toned down (tinted) to create a subdued message that is timeless and classic. This is a good color strategy to give the mark a sophisticated appearance.

HOODY NATION

Designer: Mark Raebel
Studio: Arsenal Design

Associative Color Response:
- black: powerful, strong
- high-chroma red: intense, powerful, aggressive

Color Scheme: one hue with neutral (tinted)

Often the physicality of form—the textual basis of line—is what makes the mark. There is no finer example than the Hoody Nation logomark—the splattered line work draws the audience in and holds their attention.

HOODY NATION

Designer: Mark Raebel
Studio: Arsenal Design

Associative Color Response:
- high-chroma red: brilliant, intense, energetic
- neutral gray: future, young, forward

Color Scheme: one hue with neutral and tinting

When a logotype boils down to the selection of typeface, as in the Hoody Nation mark, it is critical to discern what constitutes good anatomical structure and what does not. Most typefaces that are considered to be of quality have a stroke width-to-height ratio from 1:5 to 1:7.5; a stroke width-to-width ratio of 1:5.25 to 1:7.33; a width-to-height ratio from 0.89:1 to 1:1; and a stroke width-to-counterform ratio of 1:3.25 to 1:5.3. The "Hoody" typeface follows this rule, and is an excellent selection. Script fonts do not necessarily follow the above ratios, and in this case "Nation" does not. What makes this logotype so interesting is the opposition between the two fonts selected.

GRAFIKA 180 STUDIOS

Designer: Mark Raebel
Studio: Arsenal Design

Associative Color Response:
- black: powerful, strong
- high-chroma red: intense, powerful, aggressive

Color Scheme: one hue with shading plus neutral

Classified as a two-color job, the Grafika 180 logomark uses overprinting to create an additional third color. When using overprinting, there is no extra cost to create additional hues. This makes it an excellent way to stretch a budget.

ARMADYNE INC.

Designer: Mark Raebel
Studio: Arsenal Design

Associative Color Response:
• high-chroma orange: communication
• neutral gray: corporate, practical

Color Scheme: one hue with neutral (tinted)

The high-chroma orange and neutral gray create a well-balanced color scheme that is energetic and that communicates with subtle sophistication.

ARMADYNE INC.

Designer: Mark Raebel
Studio: Arsenal Design

Associative Color Response:
• high-chroma orange: communication, energizing, stimulating
• neutral gray: corporate, practical

Color Scheme: one hue with neutral (tinted)

When comparing Armadyne 1 and Armadyne 2, the role-reversal of the neutral gray and high-chroma orange is evident. In Armadyne 1, the neutral gray plays a predominant role within the color scheme, whereas in Armadyne 2 the high-chroma orange is the predominant color. Note how the interpretation of these two marks changes by virtue of how the hues are implemented.

KLW GROUP

Designer: Mark Raebel
Studio: Arsenal Design

Associative Color Response:
• high-chroma red-violet: sweet taste, subtle, creative
• black: powerful, basic

Color Scheme: one hue with neutral and tinting

In the KLW Group logo, a 3D illusion is achieved through warm and cool colors and scale. To exaggerate this 3D illusion, the scale of the circles, from large to small, would need to be increased, and tinting would need to be eliminated.

KLW GROUP

Designer: Mark Raebel
Studio: Arsenal Design

Associative Color Response:
• mid-range red-violet: charming
• neutral gray: quality

Color Scheme: one hue (tinted) plus neutral (tinted)

Separation through the use of color is exploited here to create a visual hierarchy.

SIT ON IT SEATING

Principal Designer: Yang Kim
Studio: BBK Studio

Associative Color Response:
- mid-range orange: inspiring
- dark red: elegant, refined
- high-chroma blue: lively, pleasing
- high-chroma yellow-green: trendy, new growth

Color Scheme: near simple analogous with tinting and shading (red); one hue with shading–monochromatic (blue and green)

In the three versions of SitOnIt Seating, cool and warm colors are used most effectively to create a 3D illusion on a 2D plane; the cool colors recede and the warm colors come forth. It is interesting to note that the 3D illusion flips back and forth from a seat to steps.

EXPRESS DIVERS

Designer: Mark Raebel
Studio: Arsenal Design

Associative Color Response:
- black: powerful, strong
- high-chroma red: intense, powerful, aggressive

Color Scheme: one hue with neutral

When using color in this manner (mostly black with an accent of red), the predominant hue dominates the interpretation. However, the most interesting part about this mark is the substitution of the diving flag for the letterform "X." Furthermore, a water wave is substituted for the airline stroke within the letterform "X." The dive flag is used when divers are out on the water. The juxtaposition of the descending diver underneath the flag puts the activity in context.

PUNK MARKETING

Studio: 86 The Onions

Associative Color Response:
- high-chroma red: aggressive, solid
- black: heavy, basic

Color Scheme: one hue plus neutral

The Punk Marketing logomark uses consistency of line and simplicity of graphics to create an aesthetically pleasing mark.

PUNK MARKETING™

NO FIELD 5

Designer: Mark Raebel
Studio: Arsenal Design

Associative Color Response:
- high-chroma red: intense, energetic
- black: powerful, strong

Color Scheme: one hue with neutral

The No Field 5 logomark is an excellent example of juxtaposing a 3D object against a flat surface to accentuate the 3D illusion.

ISLAND SPORTS

Designer: Mark Raebel
Studio: Arsenal Design

Associative Color Response:
- mid-range orange: glad, cheery
- high-chroma yellow-green: sharp, growth

Color Scheme: near incongruous

The island sports logo is a near incongruous color scheme—a highly kinetic color palette due to its chroma value. When executed properly, these offbeat color schemes tend to be unique, lively, and energetic.

NEIGHBORHOOD LAWN CARE

Designer: Mark Raebel
Studio: Arsenal Design

Associative Color Response:
- mid-range orange: glad, cheery
- dark green: natural, trustworthy

Color Scheme: two points of a triad both secondary hues with shading

Not every logo requires a high-chroma hue in the master color palette. There is no finer example of this than the Neighborhood Lawn

Care mark. As demonstrated in this book, a majority (more than 80%) of logomarks, logotypes, and symbols use high-chroma colors within their master color palette. However, one way to help create a unique mark is to find appropriate hues (that help sell or promote) that are not in the high-chroma.

STARK CERAMICS INCORPORATED

Designer/Creative Director: Drew M. Dallet
Studio: Boom Creative

Associative Color Response:
- high-chroma red: dynamic, strength
- black: powerful, strong

Color Scheme: one hue with neutral

The Stark Ceramics Incorporated logo uses four formal techniques in a most effective way to create a 3D illusion: cool and warm colors; weight; placement; and scale. The formal

execution of a mark can be likened to grammar. If grammar is used so poorly that one cannot read for content, the concept will either not be revealed, or revealed to an inadequate level. Either way, the mark or design communicates at an illiterate level.

ORDERNETWORK.COM

Art Director: Chevonne Woodard
Studio: Chevonne Woodard Design

Associative Color Response:
- high-chroma orange: communication, growing, intimate
- black: powerful, strong

Color Scheme: one hue with tinting plus neutral

This logomark is an excellent example of substitution. The indexical reference to a computer's "power on" button is a fine example of using content appropriate to the subject matter.

GAIN

Designer: Carol Chu

Associative Color Response:
- high-chroma orange: growing, energizing
- neutral gray: quality

Color Scheme: one hue plus neutral (tinted)

The Gain logo uses symbols for movement and perspective to create a mark that is highly kinetic. Within this context, an energizing high-chroma orange is used to reinforce the kinetic energy implied by the formal structure.

THE TREE HOOK

Designer: Mark Raebel
Studio: Arsenal Design

Associative Color Response:
- high-chroma blue: lively, honest, strength
- pastel blue: refreshing, clean, cool

Color Scheme: monochromatic

The tree hook logo is an excellent example of using a geometric form to unify a mark. The selection and consistency of typeface chosen also aids in this endeavor. Created from one ink, this two-color mark uses tinting to create the additional color. White (not counted as a color) is created through a type reversal in which type is knocked out to the color of the substrate.

INFO GROW

Designer/Creative Director: Drew M. Dallet
Studio: Boom Creative

Associative Color Response:
- high-chroma yellow-orange: energy, health
- high-chroma violet: memorable, thoughtful

Color Scheme: near complementary

Color offers meaning, depth, and insight into the way a company image is formed. The Info Grow logotype is a fine example of how color and shape play an important role in how a corporate image is constructed. This logo is energetic, thoughtful (color-based), and conservative (form-based).

CONGREGATION SHALOM

Designer/Creative Director: Drew M. Dallet
Studio: Boom Creative

Associative Color Response:
- high-chroma blue: dignity, calm
- gold: valuable, prestigious

Color Scheme: near complementary

The Congregation Shalom mark is a fine example of the psychological and learned behavioral effects of color. Creating the mark through the use of these two hues visually displays the values of the organization.

SWEET TOOTH FOR YOUTH

Designer/Creative Director: Drew M. Dallet
Studio: Boom Creative

Associative Color Response:
- pastel pink: soft, sweet, tender, cute
- earth-tone red: warmhearted, welcome, good, healthy

Color Scheme: near complementary

The Sweet Tooth for Youth logomark is a superb example of practical color use. The psychological and learned behavioral effects of these two hues match the content, context, and end-user beautifully. The formal anatomy of the mark also reflects the target audience—a masterful job.

HIPPOLOCO

Designer: Carol Chu

Associative Color Response:
- pastel blue-violet: flamboyant, subtle
- high-chroma orange: growing, childlike

Color Scheme: near complementary

The light and airy quality of the Hippoloco logomark can be directly contributed to the colors chosen. A hippopotamus is anything

but lightweight, however; the psychological effects of the color reinforce the humorous nature of the mark.

CELINE YALETOWN SALON

Designer: Catherine Ng
Creative Director: Carolina Becerra
Studio: Kübe Communication Design

Associative Color Response:
- neutral gray: quality, classic, professional
- high-chroma blue: electric, energetic, pleasing

Color Scheme: one hue plus neutral (tinted)

The Celine Yaletown Salon logotype uses a classic color palette with compressed lowercase letterforms to create an energetic mark with a contemporary feel.

FIREFLY

Designers: Justin Ahrens and Kerri Liu
Art Director: Justin Ahrens

Associative Color Response:
- black: powerful, elegant
- high-chroma red: hot, fire, heat

Color Scheme: one hue plus neutral

The physicality of form in the Firefly mark harmonizes with the color and typography to create a logomark that is unsurpassed by many contemporary logos.

MONARCH DESIGN & CONSTRUCTION

Designer/Art Director: Justin Ahrens

Associative Color Response:
- black: elegant, prestigious
- dark red: refined, taste

Color Scheme: one hue with shading plus neutral

The red-brick hue combined with black creates an impressive color palette suitable for the content. In this case, the red in "monarch" is an indexical reference to the way that many houses and buildings are constructed. The black hue reinforces the quality of the mark by adding power.

E-COURT

Designer: Erik Chrestensen
Studio: Chrestensen Designworks

Associative Color Response:
• black: powerful, elegant
• high-chroma red: hot, fire, heat

Color Scheme: one hue plus neutral

The E-Court logo is a fine example of hand-rendered typography and line work to create an energetic mark.

KIKUYA

Designer: Erik Chrestensen
Studio: Chrestensen Designworks

Associative Color Response:
• blue-violet: authoritative, confident, strong
• high-chroma blue: lively, strength

Color Scheme: simple analogous

The Kikuya logotype uses hand-rendered typography coupled with perspective to create a highly kinetic mark. Reversing the letterforms out of the blue-violet background makes the typography pop (warm colors come forth and cool colors recede). In this case, the substrate in which this image is printed on is critical. Placing the logo on top of a cool background will reduce the kinetic energy.

MAP STRATEGIES

Designer/Creative Director: Drew M. Dallet
Studio: Boom Creative

Associative Color Response:
• black: basic, strong
• mid-range orange: inviting, cheery

Color Scheme: one hue plus neutral

The Map Strategies mark is an excellent example of learned color response. The mark is designed after the United States Department of Motor Vehicles signage system that includes, in part, this color scheme and the shape of the sign. The letterform "S" with two arrows pointing in different directions conceptually symbolize the intent of the mark.

BLU SYNTHETIC

Designer: Dean Kujala and Carolina Becerra
Creative Director: Dean Kujala
Studio: Kübe Communication Design

Associative Color Response:
• neutral gray: quality, classic, corporate
• high-chroma blue: lively, pleasing, rich

Color Scheme: one hue plus neutral (tinted)

The Blu Synthetic logotype uses a color combination that results in a successful mark that has a corporate feel. This is brought about through the typographic relationship between "Blu" and "Synthetic," consistency of line weight, and the choice of sans-serif fonts.

TOLLAR METAL WORKS

Designer: John R. Kleinpeter
Art Director: John T. Drew

Associative Color Response:
- high-chroma blue-violet: powerful, classic
- dark red: strong, taste

Color Scheme: near incongruous or two points of a tetrad

Tollar Metal Works is a company that designs metal chairs that are used outdoors at bus and subway stops. The mark was designed to reference the three-dimensionality of the chairs and their durability. This is done through the use of two-point perspective, line weight, and cool and warm colors.

LIGHTHOUSE

Designer: Justin Deister
Studio: Uppercase Design

Associative Color Response:
- high-chroma orange: inviting
- black: powerful

Color Scheme: one hue with tinting plus neutral

The Lighthouse logomark is an excellent example of substitution and economy of form.

ANGLEBAR SOLUTIONS

Designer: Justin Deister
Studio: Uppercase Design

Associative Color Response:
- high-chroma yellow-orange: powerful, energy, drive
- high-chroma blue: mature, classy

Color Scheme: near complementary

The Anglebar Solutions logotype is a highly kinetic color scheme with a binary opposition occurring within the two fonts selected to create visual tension. Eye movement is induced whenever visual tension is created.

OH! OXYGEN

Studio: AdamsMorioka

Associative Color Response:
- neutral gray: classic, quality
- high-chroma blue: strength, lively

Color Scheme: one hue plus neutral (tinted)

Anytime a high-chroma color is used as the predominant hue, kinetic energy is induced. In this case, scale plays an important role in creating the lively Oh Oxygen logotype.

BiTiNiT

Designers: Carolina Becerra and Dean Kujala
Creative Director: Dean Kujala
Studio: Kübe Communication Design

Associative Color Response:
• high-chroma yellow-orange: drive, aggressive, powerful
• high-chroma blue: strength, work

Color Scheme: near complementary

The art of substitution is alive and well in the BiTiNiT logomark—a lively and energetic mark that uses a near complementary color palette to help express the activity in which this product is used (bits for a screw gun). A near complementary high-chroma color palette induces simultaneous contrast and heightens stimulation within the eye (the photoreceptor cells responsible for detecting blue and yellow-orange fire with force, creating more stimulation).

WATKINS COLLEGE OF ART & DESIGN

Designer: Leslie Haines

Associative Color Response:
• high-chroma orange: energizing, pride
• high-chroma blue: lively, pleasing

Color Scheme: direct complementary

Direct complementary color schemes typically create high-energy marks. This can be attributed to simultaneous contrast, high-chroma color palettes, and a greater stimulation of the photoreceptor cells found within the eye.

KÜBE

Studio: Kübe Communication Design

Associative Color Response:
• dark gray: wise, professional
• high-chroma yellow-orange: drive, goal, enterprise

Color Scheme: one hue plus neutral (tinted)

Typically when a dark gray is used within a logotype, such as Kübe, a professional, corporate feel is induced. This works well with standardized type—typefaces consisting of the proper stroke width-to-width ratio, stroke width-to-height ratio, and stroke width-to-counterform ratio. A high-chroma yellow-orange is used as an accent color to help energize the mark.

NEXUS

Studio: Kübe Communication Design

Associative Color Response:
• neutral gray: classic, quality
• high-chroma red: power, stimulating

Color Scheme: one hue plus neutral (tinted)

A neutral gray and high-chroma red color scheme has a classic appearance. This color combination tends to yield a lively yet conservative color palette.

SULING

Designer: Suling Pong

Associative Color Response:
• black: powerful, elegant
• dark red: mature, serious

Color Scheme: one hue with shading plus neutral

In the Suling logomark, the line weight of the outer line harmonizes well with the font used. A dark red and black color scheme further induces a harmonious relationship, with black added to the red to darken it (shading).

CARLEY SPARKS

Studio: Sharp Pixel

Associative Color Response:
• black: powerful, strong
• high-chroma pink: exciting, stimulating, aggressive
• pastel pink: joyful, active, energetic, subtle

Color Scheme: one hue with tinting plus neutral (high-chroma pink); monochromatic with tinting and shading (pastel pink)

The top Carley Sparks logo is an excellent example of using ingredients in a unique way to induce kinetic energy. In this case, the gradients help to create a 3D illusion on a 2D plane that activate the mark. The pastel logo is a fine example of a subdued mark brought about through tinting and shading. Note the difference between the scheme in the top logo and this color scheme—each induces a different psychological effect on the viewer.

CDLS FOUNDATION

Designer: Laurie Churchman
Studio: Designlore

Associative Color Response:
• blue-purple: tender, classic
• blue-green: pristine, pure

Color Scheme: two points of a split complementary

This logo has a unique color scheme that helps communicate the values of the CdLS Foundation. The mark is superbly executed; it is a wonderful example of economy of line.

SUNSAFE

Studio: AdamsMorioka

Associative Color Response:
• high-chroma yellow-orange: fun, excitement
• high-chroma blue: lively, energetic

Color Scheme: near complementary

In this logo, both the color palette chosen and the line work surrounding the capital letterform "S" energize the mark.

EVD 4x4

Studio: 86 The Onions

Associative Color Response:
• high-chroma orange: energizing, hot
• neutral gray: quality, passion

Color Scheme: one hue plus neutral (tinted)

The EVD 4x4 logomark uses a conservative color scheme with a typeface that has a bold thick-to-thin relationship that helps to induce kinetic energy.

EOS AIRLINES

Studio: Hornall Anderson Design Works

Associative Color Response:
• high-chroma yellow-orange: luxurious, cheery
• pastel blue: clean, calm

Color Scheme: near complementary with shading and tinting

This logotype is an excellent example of understanding typographic anatomy in relationship to motion. The letterforms are extended so that the counterforms are five times wider than the stroke, or a 1:7 stroke width-to-width ratio. The typeface has a moderate thick-to-thin relationship, allowing for excellent legibility at a distance—the thinnest part of the letterforms will disappear first. On the tail section of the airplane, the logotype is reversed out to white through a dark blue-violet, allowing for excellent legibility at a distance in daylight.

CLEARWIRE

Studio: Hornall Anderson Design Works

Associative Color Response:
• high-chroma blue-violet: classic, powerful
• high-chroma yellow-green: strength, sharp

Color Scheme: two points of the triad/near incongruous

The color scheme chosen for the Clear Wire logotype reinforces the company's mission statement. Gestalt is used within the lowercase letterform "i," further strengthening the conceptual metaphor.

clearw re

ADAMSMORIOKA

Studio: AdamsMorioka

Associative Color Response:
• high-chroma red: dignity, power
• black: elegant, powerful

Color Scheme: one hue plus neutral

The AdamsMorioka logo is a superb example of a conservative color scheme coupled with a classical typeface (stroke width-to-height ratio 1:6.25, stroke width-to-width ratio 1:5.25, width-to-height ratio .84:1, and stroke width-to-counterform ratio 1:3.25). A minimum of substitution is used, creating a classically restrained and sophisticated mark.

AdamsMorioka

INSITE WORKS

Studio: Hornall Anderson Design Works

Associative Color Response:
- high-chroma orange: producing, communication
- high-chroma blue-violet: powerful, expensive

Color Scheme: near complementary

The logotype for Insite Works uses a high-chroma, near complementary color scheme to energize a typically staid industry.

VECTOR

Studio: Hornall Anderson Design Works

Associative Color Response:
- high-chroma blue: dramatic, electric
- high-chroma blue-violet: powerful, expensive

Color Scheme: simple analogous

The Vector logomark uses a simple analogous color palette to counterbalance the highly active formal relationships found within the mark. This type of color palette helps to unify a mark. If this was a direct complementary or near complementary color palette, the mark would appear to be fragmented.

ALLCONNECT

Studio: Hornall Anderson Design Works

Associative Color Response:
- earth tone: warm, durable, secure
- high-chroma yellow-green: strength

Color Scheme: two points of a split complementary with shading and tinting

In the allconnect logotype, substitution and separation are used to create a highly effective mark. The "power-on" symbol is substituted for the "o" in "connect" to metaphorically represent the company. Separation is used (a formal technique to clearly distinguish the most meaningful part or parts) by use of cool and warm colors. The yellow-green hue represents not only "power on" (learned behavioral association), but also visually separates the word "on" from "connect."

SUNDANCE INSTITUTE

Studio: AdamsMorioka

Associative Color Response:
- high-chroma orange: dramatic, energetic
- black: powerful, strength

Color Scheme: one hue plus neutral

The choice of font, color scheme, and placement of type and color in the Sundance Institute logotype is designed to give the mark stability. The typeface chosen is an expanded face, giving the mark a longer horizon line. This is amplified by the amount of tracking used. The black hue is employed, as a foundation, for Sundance to set upon—further adding stability. Finally, the type is arranged symmetrically to further amplify this notion.

SEATTLE'S CONVENTION AND VISITORS BUREAU

Studio: Hornall Anderson Design Works

Associative Color Response:
- mid-range green: classic
- black: powerful, strength

Color Scheme: one hue plus neutral

The color black in the Seattle's Convention and Visitors Bureau mark is primarily used to unify the mark. The mid-range green is used to humanize the symbol.

KO:KE

Designer: Zeljka Zupanic

Associative Color Response:
- high-chroma yellow-orange: stimulating, cheerful
- black: powerful, strength

Color Scheme: one hue plus neutral

The KO:KE logomark use of one hue with a neutral color is symmetrically balanced to give the mark authority.

FUNNY BOY FILMS

Designers: Shaun Webb, James Sakamoto, and Matt Sloane
Art Director: Mark Sackett
Studio: Sackett Design

Associative Color Response:
- mid-range green: stimulating, cheerful
- black: powerful, strength

Color Scheme: one hue plus neutral

The method of separation (i.e., marking out plainly the most meaningful part) is used within the Funny Boy Films logotype. In this method, four formal techniques are used to help create a jumping sensation: 3D illusion; extra fat-to-skinny; flipped typography; and tilting a letterform off the pre-existing plane. When added up, this logotype constitutes a lively and energetic mark.

COMMUNITIES.COM

Designer: Mark Sackett

Associative Color Response:
- high-chroma blue-violet: classic, powerful
- black: powerful, strength

Color Scheme: one hue plus neutral

The communities.com logotype uses similarity of form to harmonize all parts. The dot at the end of "communities" is the exact size of the eye of the lowercase "i." The dot is then enlarged to be utilized as a balloon. Blue-violet is used in the enlarged dot as if it were an inflection in someone's voice.

TERRAVIDA COFFEE

Studio: Hornall Anderson Design Works

Associative Color Response:
- high-chroma orange: tasty, warm
- black: powerful, strength

Color Scheme: one hue plus neutral

Texture and substitution is used in the TerraVida Coffee logo to create visual appeal. Texture acts as a visual magnet—it draws

the viewer in. The modified "A" and "V" in TerraVida use the idea of a leaf or coffee bean to attract visual interest.

MAD CHINAMAN

Designer: Audrey Koh
Studio: Plastic Soldier Factory Pte Ltd

Associative Color Response:
- high-chroma orange: dramatic, energetic
- high-chroma blue: electric, vibrant

Color Scheme: direct complementary

Pronounced simultaneous contrast occurs when there is an imbalance in the proportion of two hues on the opposite side of the color

wheel (large to small). Such is the case in this mark design by Audrey Koh. Pronounced simultaneous contrast induces a strobing effect caused by the receptor cells responsible for detecting color.

SAN FRANCISCO MARRIOTT

Studio: Hornall Anderson Design Works

Associative Color Response:
- dark yellow: flavorsome
- golden-yellow: pleasant, harvest, natural

Color Scheme: one hue with shading (achromatic)

Due to the color palette chosen, the San Francisco Marriott mark is warm, inviting, and restful. The symmetrical balance further amplifies this feel.

VIRTUTECH

Studio: Hornall Anderson Design Works

Associative Color Response:
- neutral gray: flavorsome
- high-chroma orange: pleasant, harvest, natural

Color Scheme: one hue plus neutral (tinted)

Any time a warm, high-chroma hue is juxtaposed next to a neutral gray, the color will pop. This is the case with the high-chroma orange in the virtutech logomark—it appears to jump forward.

CENTENAL

Designer: Tanya A. Ortega
Art Director: John T. Drew

Associative Color Response:
- high-chroma red-violet: exciting, flamboyant
- high-chroma blue: lively, dramatic

Color Scheme: two points of a tetrad (near incongruous)

This modular-system logomark uses an offbeat color combination to create a vibrant and kinetic mark. High-chroma hues coupled with a directional mark (spinning) allow the typography in the Centenal mark to interlock.

SCREAMER

Studio: Hornall Anderson Design Works

Associative Color Response:
- neutral blue-gray: mature, solid
- high-chroma orange: harvest, natural

Color Scheme: one hue plus neutral (tinted)

The Screamer logomark is a fine example of using warm and cool colors to make the mark pop off the page.

RIVER PLACE

Studio: Hornall Anderson Design Works

Associative Color Response:
- olive: natural
- high-chroma blue: calm, relaxed

Color Scheme: one hue plus neutral

The high-chroma, blue-and-olive color scheme is a fine example of both learned association and psychological understanding.

CENTRAAL MUSEUM

Studio: Thonik Design

Associative Color Response:
- high-chroma green: hope, lively
- high-chroma blue-violet: powerful, fantasy

Color Scheme: two points of a tetrad

This offbeat color combination harmonizes through the use of cyan. The mark consists of a bold graphic shape with a lowercase letterform "c" stepped and repeated to create a modular mark.

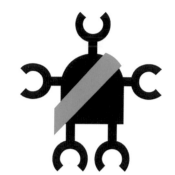

CENTRAAL MUSEUM: NEO

Studio: Thonik Design

Associative Color Response:
- high-chroma pink: aggressive, exciting
- high-chroma yellow: vigorous, youthful

Color Scheme: incongruous

The Neo logomark uses a high-chroma color palette to help create a highly kinetic mark. Part of a series (see left), the lowercase letterform "c" is utilized again to create visual consistency from mark to mark, as well as to induce kinetic energy through placement and scaling.

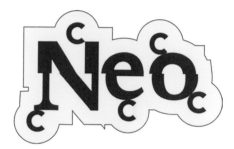

MOCHA BEES

Designer: Tanya A. Ortega
Art Director: John T. Drew

Associative Color Response:
- earth-tone red: wholesome, good, healthy
- golden yellow: harvest, natural

Color Scheme: two points of a Tetrad

The hues chosen for this mark were based on learned color identification (milk chocolate and honey). Tinting the hue to give it a more favorable appetite rating toned down the honey color.

FULL MOON FOODS

Designer: Wayne Sakamoto
Art Director: Mark Sackett
Studio: Sackett Design

Associative Color Response:
- golden-yellow/beige: dignified, buttery
- high-chroma blue-violet: regal, classic

Color Scheme: direct complementary with tinting and shading

The Full Moon Foods logomark is an excellent example of using the right hues for food products. The golden-yellow hue suggests baked goods, whereas the blue-violet when juxtaposed with fruit causes the warm colors of the fruit to pop.

TEGA

Designer: Tanya A. Ortega
Art Director: John T. Drew

Associative Color Response:
• neutral gray: classic, timeless, practical
• dark gray: solid, classic

Color Scheme: achromatic

This color palette creates a highly professional and subdued logomark for a fishing outfitter. Focusing on quality, a reductive illustration was created using shades of gray to reinforce the idea.

XILOX

Designer: Tanya A. Ortega
Art Director: John T. Drew

Associative Color Response:
• high-chroma red: brilliant, energizing
• black: powerful, elegant

Color Scheme: one hue plus neutral

The Xilox logomark is an excellent example of a modular system—the mark consists of two repeating parts. Red and black make an energetic color scheme that creates a highly kinetic experience in combination with the mark. The mark is placed on an angle to help induce kinetic energy by creating visual tension with the company name—an oppositional technique. This color scheme is highly energetic. A high-chroma red hue is intensely vivid and warm and moves forward to more than most warm colors. The black hue is very cool, in opposition to the red hue.

STAGE

Designer: Tanya A. Ortega
Art Director: John T. Drew

Associative Color Response:
• high-chroma red: brilliant, energizing
• black: powerful, elegant

Color Scheme: one hue plus neutral

Red-and-black color schemes work well for inducing kinetic energy or for activating a mark. (See Xilox, above.)

DOREE

Designer: Tarun Deep Girdher

Associative Color Response:
• high-chroma red: brilliant, energizing
• high-chroma blue: lively, pleasing

Color Scheme: primary

Within this mark, the high-chroma hues are used to energize the logo and make it harmonize with the typographic forms.

YES

Designer: Stefan G. Bucher
Studio: 344

Associative Color Response:
• high-chroma red: brilliant, energizing
• high-chroma orange: lively, pleasing

Color Scheme: two points of the split complementary

The #Yes logomark uses a warm color palette in combination with perspective to create an intriguing mark that looks 3D.

ROCKRIDGE

Designer: Brenda Spivack
Studio: Red Table

Associative Color Response:
• neutral: quality
• high-chroma blue-violet: classic

Color Scheme: one hue plus neutral (tinted)

This combination of typeface and color palette creates a classic and timeless logotype.

ROCKRIDGE

Designer: Carlo Irgoyen
Art Director: Brenda Spivack
Studio: Red Table

Associative Color Response:
• light gray: cool, classic
• neutral gray: corporate, timeless

Color Scheme: simple achromatic

The Rockridge logotype is a fine example of using gestalt to create an identifiable mark (double R).

ROCKRIDGE

Designer/Art Director: Scott Pridgen

Associative Color Response:
• earth-tone red: rustic, warm
• neutral gray: corporate, timeless

Color Scheme: one hue with tinting and shading plus neutral (tinted)

This logo in the Rockridge series uses the font Copperplate coupled with the earth tone and neutral gray color scheme to communicate a rustic feel.

BAGIRNA

Designer/Art Director: Scott Pridgen

Associative Color Response:
• high-chroma red-violet: cool, classic
• high-chroma yellow-green: corporate, timeless

Color Scheme: near/direct complementary

The Bagirna logotype is a superbly executed retro mark that uses substitution in a clever and intriguing way. The direct complementary, high-chroma color palette helps communicate the psychedelic nature of the mark.

K&G

Designer: Carlo Irgoyen
Art Director: Brenda Spivack
Studio: Red Table

Associative Color Response:
• pastel green: smooth, quiet
• warm neutral gray: corporate, timeless

Color Scheme: one hue plus neutral (tinted)

The form/counterform relationship found within the K&G logotype is superbly executed to create a cohesive whole. The muted color palette softens the capitalized letterforms to create a conservative corporate feel.

HOOPNOTICA

Designer: Carlo Irgoyen
Art Director: Brenda Spivack
Studio: Red Table

Associative Color Response:
• high-chroma pink: stimulating, exciting
• high-chroma red-violet: feminine, flamboyant

Color Scheme: simple analogous

The high-chroma hues used in this logomark create an atmosphere that is highly dynamic and filled with kinetic energy.

CITY BEVERAGE

Designer/Art Director: Scott Pridgen

Associative Color Response:
• mid-range red-purple: charming, refined
• high-chroma red-violet: sweet taste, exciting

Color Scheme: monochromatic with tinting

The City Beverage logotype uses typographic opposition to create a visually intriguing mark. The monochromatic color scheme is used to unify the mark.

JOEL CONFER

Designer/Illustrator/Art Director:
Lanny Sommese
Studio: Sommese Design

Associative Color Response:
• high-chroma pink: stimulating, fun
• black: spiritual, basic

Color Scheme: one hue plus neutral

As noted in most of the two-color logomarks illustrated in this chapter, the black hue is used with an additional color. This color is typically on the warm side of the color wheel, helping to make the mark pop or stand out. This is the case with the Joel Confer logo.

WAITER

Designer/Illustrator/Art Director:
Lanny Sommese
Studio: Sommese Design

Associative Color Response:
• high-chroma red: energizing, dramatic
• black: elegant, night

Color Scheme: one hue plus neutral

The master of substitution, designer and
illustrator Lanny Sommese, illustrates the art
of camouflage and deception within this mark.

The counterform of the center forearm creates
a waiter's face. This is a wonderfully executed
example of economy of line.

2004 PET EXTRAVAGANZA

Designer/Illustrator/Art Director:
Lanny Sommese
Studio: Sommese Design

Associative Color Response:
• high-chroma green: new growth
• black: prestigious, spiritual, basic

Color Scheme: one hue plus neutral

The 2004 Pet Extravaganza logomark creates
a form/counterform relationship that unites
the two halves of the mark. The high-chroma
green is used, through the use of learned
association, as representative of grass.

TECNOKAR

Designer/Art Director: Scott Pridgen

Associative Color Response:
• high-chroma blue: work, strong
• black: powerful, heavy

Color Scheme: one hue plus neutral

The use of the blue hue (cool color) in the
Tecnokar logo helps articulate a 3D illusion.
This is also achieved through perspective
and opposition with the company name.

MT

Designer: Mike Paz
Art Director: John T. Drew

Associative Color Response:
• high-chroma orange: thought, receptive
• high-chroma yellow-orange: enterprise,
  powerful

Color Scheme: simple analogous

This logotype is a beautiful combination
of color, gestalt, and economy of line. Note
how the stroke of the capital letterform "M" is
perfectly executed by placing the counterform
at the right distance away from the "t." The
color scheme, which is simple analogous,
perfectly matches the elegant execution of
this logotype.

VYWAY MARKET & BRAND STRATEGY

Designer: Renita Breitenbucher
Studio: Nita B. Creative

Associative Color Response:
• high-chroma blue: lively, pleasing
• neutral gray: classic, corporate, timeless

Color Scheme: one hue plus neutral (tinted)

The Vyway Market & Brand Strategy mark demonstrates the simplicity of a well-executed design. The color scheme is well chosen to communicate a professional atmosphere.

GULLIFTY'S

Designer/Art Director: Lanny Sommese
Calligrapher: Bill Kinser
Studio: Sommese Design

Associative Color Response:
• high-chroma green: life, fresh
• golden yellow: dignified, pleasant

Color Scheme: near incongruous

The unusual color palette chosen for the Gullifty's logomark demonstrates the uniqueness of incongruous color schemes. If done well, these types of color palettes can infuse marks with lively interplay.

THE SALOON

Designer: Kristin Sommese
Art Directors: Kristin Sommese
and Lanny Sommese
Studio: Sommese Design

Associative Color Response:
• high-chroma yellow: agreeable,
  pleasant, youthful
• black: powerful, heavy, basic

Color Scheme: one hue plus neutral

Often, overlapping objects induce kinetic energy—this is the case with The Saloon logomark. Note how the beer mug is moving into the circle. A large portion of the beer mug is within the circle, while a small part is outside. This causes the beer mug image to move in an inward direction; it is also helped by the way the object is drawn. If a greater part of the image were placed outside of the circle, no matter how the object was drawn, the object would move in an outward direction.

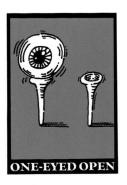

ONE-EYED OPEN

Designer/Illustrator/Art Director:
Lanny Sommese
Studio: Sommese Design

Associative Color Response:
• high-chroma green: nervous, grass
• black: powerful, basic

Color Scheme: one hue plus neutral

The One-Eyed Open logomark uses learned color association to help place this mark in context. This humorous mark references the human anatomy, not only the eyeball but also by the placement of the two golf tees.

SAFE CHICAGO

Designer: Michael Gray

Associative Color Response:
- high-chroma red: hoping, warm
- black: powerful, basic

Color Scheme: one hue plus neutral

This mark is an excellent example of economy of line. The red cross is perfectly positioned so that the top section also functions as the front door. The color red is symbolically used to communicate a welcome hope.

BEAR'S KITCHEN

Designer: Minato Ishikawa

Associative Color Response:
- high-chroma red: hoping, warm
- high-chroma blue: powerful, basic

Color Scheme: primary

Here, quality of line work coupled with the primary color palette is superbly geared toward the target audience (children).

NITA B. CREATIVE

Designer: Renita Breitenbucher
Studio: Nita B. Creative

Associative Color Response:
- elegant: black
- high-chroma blue: dignity, pleasing, mature

Color Scheme: simple monochromatic plus neutral

This simple monochromatic study (two steps) with a neutral (black hue) is executed to convey elegance. This is brought about through the color choice, typeface, and geometric forms.

IR

Designer: Alex Prompongsatorn
Art Director: John T. Drew

Associative Color Response:
- high-chroma red: stimulating, active
- pastel blue: pleasure, refreshing

Color Scheme: primary with tinting

Here, the economy of line, form/counterform relationship, and outlined letterforms create a highly kinetic logotype. The primary color palette further amplifies the kinetic energy of this mark.

SOMMESE POSTERS

Designer/Illustrator/Art Director:
Lanny Sommese
Studio: Sommese Design

Associative Color Response:
• high-chroma yellow: cheerful, youthful
• black: powerful

Color Scheme: one hue plus neutral

The Sommese Posters mark combines
a high-chroma hue (yellow) and type
as image to create a human face.

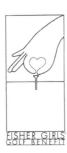

FISHER GIRLS' GOLF BENEFIT

Designer/Illustrator: Lanny Sommese
Art Directors: Kristin Sommese
and Lanny Sommese
Studio: Sommese Design

Associative Color Response:
• high-chroma yellow: cheerful, youthful
• black: powerful

Color Scheme: one hue accent plus neutral

The Fisher Girls' Golf Benefit uses substitution
in a most elegant way. Separation, achieved
through the use of color, highlights the most
meaningful part.

SOMMESE DESIGN

Designer/Illustrator/Art Director:
Lanny Sommese
Studio: Sommese Design

Associative Color Response:
• high-chroma red: cheerful, curious
• dark orange: provoking, stimulating

Color Scheme: simple analogous with
tinting and shading

This male/female mark uses a simple
analogous color palette to help communicate
a humorous yet tasteful mark.

NS

Designer: Jessica L. Howard
Art Director: John T. Drew

Associative Color Response:
• high-chroma blue-green: cheerful, curious
• dark blue: provoking, stimulating

Color Scheme: simple analogous with tinting
and shading

The blue hue within the NS logotype uses
shading to create the darker color and tinting
to lighten the hue up a little. This hue is
juxtaposed next to the high-chroma blue-
green hue to create a dynamic simple
analogous (two steps) color palette. These two
hues are used to create a visual separation
between the capital letterforms "N" and "S."

LOVE POLLUTION

Designer: Betty Avila
Art Director: John T. Drew

Associative Color Response:
• high-chroma red: love, compassion
• dark gray: debase

Color Scheme: one hue with neutral (tinted)

Substitution and color coding is used in the love Pollution logomark to create a wonderful masthead. Both the dark gray and high-chroma red uses learned color association to execute the concept.

love
Pollution

ALEX DESIGN

Designer: Alex Prompongsatorn
Art Director: John T. Drew

Associative Color Response:
• pastel blue: lively, strong
• mid-range pink: restrained

Color Scheme: primary with tinting

This modular-system mark uses a blue dot placed in the center that is exactly one-half the thickness of the stroke adjacent to it. This ensures that the dot harmonizes with the two adjacent elements.

SAVANNAH HILL

Designer/Illustrator/Art Director:
Lanny Sommese
Studio: Sommese Design

Associative Color Response:
• pastel pink: comfortable, romantic
• high-chroma blue-green: paradise, pure

Color Scheme: near complementary with tinting

The color combination for the Savannah Hills mark uses learned color association to help communicate a tropical paradise. This is also brought about through the form and silhouette of the object used.

Savannah Hill

KENNEY YANG

Designer: Kenney Yang

Associative Color Response:
• black: powerful, strong
• neutral gray: corporate, quality

Color Scheme: simple achromatic

If done correctly, when using a modular system to create a logomark, consistency at all levels of business operations is implied. In this case, the choice of color palette communicates quality.

**KENNEY
YANG**

FACULTY OF ARTS AND SCIENCES: RUTGERS UNIVERSITY NEWARK

Designer/Art Director: Ned Drew

Associative Color Response:
• black: elegant
• high-chroma red: brilliant

Color Scheme: one hue with neutral

The economy of line found within the logotype is superbly executed. Note how the top spine of the "s" and the bowl of the lowercase "a" are used as one element to communicate both letterforms. The sophistication of this logotype, coupled with the red-and-black color combination, communicates content and context.

THE DESIGN CONSORTIUM

Designer/Art Director: Ned Drew

Associative Color Response:
• neutral gray: quality
• high-chroma red: energizing

Color Scheme: one hue with neutral

A student graphic studio, Rutgers University (The State University of New Jersey, Newark) Design Consortium presents enthusiasm with a polished finish in their logomark. The color choice creates a 3D effect while being mindful of the studio's well-respected and award-winning design status.

GRAPHIC INSTINCT

Designer: Linda Liejard

Associative Color Response:
• black: elegant, strong
• high-chroma red: brilliant

Color Scheme: one hue with neutral

Economy of line is one of the most effective ways to create a logotype. The Graphic Instinct mark is a fine example of this.

I-COPACK

Designer: Linda Liejard

Associative Color Response:
• dark yellow: active
• high-chroma red-orange: energizing, stimulating

Color Scheme: near incongruous with shading

These types of color palettes are used less often and therefore offer a more unusual color appearance. A near incongruous, or two points of a tetrad, color palette is less likely to clash than a straight-up incongruous color scheme.

RICHIE H. EAP

Designer: Richie H. Eap
Art Director: John T. Drew

Associative Color Response:
- high-chroma orange: active
- high-chroma blue-violet: energizing, stimulating

Color Scheme: near complementary

In the Richie H. Eap personal logotype, note how the top bowl of the lowercase "e" and the arm of the lowercase "r" line to create a unified mark. A complementary color palette is used to help activate the composition.

RICHIE H. EAP

Designer: Richie H. Eap
Art Director: John T. Drew

Associative Color Response:
- high-chroma yellow-green: active
- high-chroma violet: energizing, stimulating

Color Scheme: near complementary

An excellent example of substitution, designer Richie H. Eap supplants a lowercase "r" for the stem of the Uppercase "E." He further uses substitution by replacing the arm of the uppercase "E" with a tilde sign found within the same typeface. This ensures visual consistency. A near complementary color scheme is used to activate the mark.

APS CORPORATION

Designer: Linda Liejard

Associative Color Response:
- high-chroma blue: dignity
- high-chroma orange: friendly

Color Scheme: near complementary

By placing the mark on an angle and using a high-chroma near complementary color palette, the mark becomes energized.

APS is separated from the rest of the mark by placing it on a horizontal angle (it is broken from the pre-existing plane). This draws the eye toward it and calls forth the most meaningful part of the mark.

WU DESIGN

Designer: Songlin Wu
Art Director: John T. Drew

Associative Color Response:
- high-chroma blue: dignified, relaxed
- pastel blue: calm, quiet

Color Scheme: simple monochromatic with tinting

The mark produced by Songlin Wu is an excellent example of a modular system. A simple, monochromatic color palette with tinting is used to help create a 3D illusion on a 2D plane.

ADVENTURE TRAVEL GROUP

Designer/Art Director: Saied Farisi

Associative Color Response:
• high-chroma red: energetic
• black: elegant, mysterious

Color Scheme: one hue plus neutral

The mark that is displayed within this logomark is perfectly symmetrical. To ensure that all anatomical parts are a mirror to one another, execute only one half of the mark, then copy, place, and flip the mark into position.

BUREAU OF PRIMARY CARE AND RURAL HEALTH SYSTEMS

Designer/Art Director: Saied Farisi

Associative Color Response:
• earth-tone red: warm, secure
• black: elegant

Color Scheme: one hue (shaded) plus neutral

The rectangle used in this logomark references the State in which this bureau operates; the flower depicted within the rectangle is indigenous to the region; and the color palette is coded to the landscape (inter-mountain west of the United States).

BUREAU OF PRIMARY CARE AND RURAL HEALTH SYSTEMS

Designer/Art Director: Saied Farisi

Associative Color Response:
• high-chroma orange: healing
• high-chroma blue-green: pure

Color Scheme: near complementary with shading

Note how the flower is primarily inside of the rectangle, implying that this species of flower is indigenous to the geographical location (inter-mountain West of the United States).

ARTISTRY NAILS

Designer: Linda Liejard

Associative Color Response:
• high-chroma yellow-green: bold
• high-chroma pink: stimulating

Color Scheme: near complementary with tinting

Simplicity of line and effective color use and placement unifies the four components found within the mark. A near complementary color palette is used to create a lively color scheme.

BIKE U.S.A.

Designer: Andrew Ung
Art Director: John T. Drew

Associative Color Response:
• high-chroma red: brilliant, energizing
• high-chroma blue: honesty, strength

Color Scheme: incongruous

The logotype created for bike u.s.a. is an excellent example of learned color association. Patriotic in its theme, this logotype is an excellent example of type as image.

WARD ENGINEERING GROUP

Designer/Art Director: Saied Farisi

Associative Color Response:
- high-chroma red: brilliant, energizing
- high-chroma blue-violet: power, dignified

Color Scheme: two points of a split complementary

This highly energetic color combination infuses vigor into a mark that already has kinetic energy. By doing so, a 3D penetrating effect is created.

ASPIRE

Creative Director: David Ferrell

Associative Color Response:
- dark gray: endearing
- neutral gray: quality, passion

Color Scheme: simple monochromatic with tinting

The aspire logotype uses a gradient to metaphorically symbolize the meaning of the word. The font chosen is a very open counterform typeface to help reinforce the concept. The logotype is beautifully simple.

FLUX

Designer: Diana Gonzalez
Art Director: Jen Bracy

Associative Color Response:
- high-chroma red: energetic
- black: powerful, strong

Color Scheme: one hue plus neutral

The formal execution and the applied color use is an excellent example of the literal meaning of the word. This superbly executed mark clearly demonstrates how color can be used in the creation of content.

APS CORPORATION

Designer: Linda Liejard

Associative Color Response:
- dark yellow: active

Color Scheme: simple monochromatic

The APS mark is a fine example of the phenomenon that cool colors recede and warm colors come forth. A simple monochromatic color study is used to help articulate the 3D illusion. Tinting is applied to the two shapes that appear to be in front. If this color solution were reversed, the mark would appear to be flat.

APS CORP.

GR

Designer: Songlin Wu
Art Director: John T. Drew

Associative Color Response:
- high-chroma blue: pleasing, lively
- pastel blue: refreshing, dependable

Color Scheme: simple monochromatic with tinting

The similarity of form (five circles) in the logotype act to unify the mark, and the simple monochromatic color palette is used to help establish a visual hierarchy.

CHICAGO CHILDREN'S CHOIR

Studio: Essex Two

Associative Color Response:
• high-chroma red: energizing
• black: strong, basic

Color Scheme: one hue plus neutral

Separation and consistency of form help
to create this unified mark.

IROX

Designer: April Medina

Associative Color Response:
• high-chroma red: energizing
• black: strong, basic

Color Scheme: one hue plus neutral

When using any color combination, a more
dynamic color palette can often be created
when there is an imbalance of hues, as
shown here.

RHOMBUS TECHNOLOGIES

Designer/Art Director: Saied Farisi

Associative Color Response:
• high-chroma red: energizing
• black: strong, basic

Color Scheme: one hue plus neutral

The practical use of color is often
overlooked. The way that the color
is placed within this mark creates eye
movement in a positive direction.

HETRICK COMMUNICATIONS

Studio: Essex Two

Associative Color Response:
• high-chroma red: energizing
• black: strong, basic

Color Scheme: one hue plus neutral

An imbalance in color here helps to create
a dynamic logotype. Placing the capital
"H" on an angle helps to further induce
kinetic energy.

ICIN

Studio: Essex Two

Associative Color Response:
- high-chroma blue: lively
- black: powerful, strong, basic

Color Scheme: one hue plus neutral

This modular system is an excellent example of using separation to create a figure/ground relationship within a mark. The blue modular unit is separated and placed in a different hue that is lighter than the four other units. This gives the impression that this is the top right portion of the mark.

CAMP MADRON

Studio: Essex Two

Associative Color Response:
- dark red: earthy, strong
- earth-tone red: rustic, earthy

Color Scheme: simple achromatic

The simple achromatic color scheme employed within this mark harmonizes with the aesthetic form. This includes using a dark red and earth-tone red hue.

EQUITY RESIDENTIAL

Studio: Essex Two

Associative Color Response:
- dark red: elegant, refined
- black: powerful, strong

Color Scheme: one hue plus neutral

Any time a flat object is juxtaposed with an object that looks 3D, both objects will amplify their corresponding effects.

BURACK & CO

Studio: Essex Two

Associative Color Response:
- high-chroma green: springtime, life
- high-chroma blue: happy, dramatic

Color Scheme: two points of a split complementary

A near simple analogous color palette, or two points of a split complementary, this mark uses the color scheme to its full potential. The green hue is lighter than the blue, creating a foreground/background relationship.

Three Colors

A true three-color logomark, using three inks, is rare in comparison with all other marks. A three-color mark offers little budgetary gain and is far more expensive than a one- or two-color mark. Therefore, stretching two colors to make them look like three is often a better solution. Many of the logos found in this chapter do just that, or use a four-color process to build a three-hue color combination.

Many of the traditional color schemes that have been empirically tested by generations use three hues. Primary, secondary, tertiary, triadic, split complementary, and an analogous color scheme use three hues to construct the palette. However, many of the traditional color palettes that use two hues can be easily altered to create a complex color scheme. Within this chapter there are excellent examples of color use and color management. From budgetary concerns to legibility issues, color ultimately controls the effectiveness of the end product.

LION

Designer: Chihiro Katoh

Associative Color Response:
- high-chroma red-orange: healing, growing, happy
- dark orange: exhilarating, inspiring, stimulating
- mid-range pink: restrained, soft, quiet

Color Scheme: near analogous plus tint

POLAR BEAR

Designer: Chihiro Katoh

Associative Color Response:
- high-chroma blue-violet: charming, refined
- dark blue: serene, credible, devoted
- mid-range blue-violet: elegant

Color Scheme: monochromatic (plus tint and shade)

GIRAFFE

Designer: Chihiro Katoh

Associative Color Response:
- high-chroma orange: healing, growing, happy
- dark orange: exhilarating, inspiring, stimulating
- pastel orange: gentle

Color Scheme: monochromatic (plus tint and shade)

ALLIGATOR

Designer: Chihiro Katoh

Associative Color Response:
- high-chroma green: life, motion, growth
- dark green: natural, growth, restful
- pastel green: classic

Color Scheme: monochromatic (plus tint and shade)

These four marks are unified through the use of an overriding tetrad color scheme (red, blue, orange, green). Each mark uses its primary color as a point of departure to define additional analogous or monochromatic hues. In this way, the designer achieves unity within each mark and creates an overall playful identity that would work well for children.

ENVENT, INC. (ENT)

Designer: Francisco Ortiz
Art Director: John T. Drew

Associative Color Response:
- gold: valuable
- high-chroma blue: dignity
- neutral gray: quality

Color Scheme: incongruous plus
neutral (tinted)

The planes of color build letter recognition
from left to right. The prominent white "e"
serves as a wayfinding tool that defines the
starting point, further reiterated in the thin
line that unifies the mark and connotes
the minimal characteristics of each letter.
In the examples shown here, the foreground,
background, and the movement between
these areas are created through the change
of line quality in both of these marks. What
makes each of them distinctive is the subtle
connotations implied by the quality of the line
(organic versus inorganic).

DASH

Studio: Bremmer & Goris Communications

Associative Color Response:
- high-chroma yellow: agreeable
- high-chroma blue: lively
- high-chroma green: motion

Color Scheme: random/primaries and
secondary hues

The negative white lines of this logomark
build layers of information from foreground
to background through variable thicknesses.

The lines become thick and bolder in the
foreground and diminish to a thin horizon line.
This basic design concept is strengthened
through the use of pure colors that activate
the eye and reinforce the directional quality
inherent in the mark.

TERMETUHELJ

Designer: Izvorka Serdarevic
Studio: Tridvajedan

Associative Color Response:
- high-chroma blue: lively, pleasant
- high-chroma yellow-green: new growth, sharp
- black: powerful, basic

Color Scheme: near incongruous

The Terme Tuhelj logomark was designed
for a natural-spring spa in the inner part of
Croatia (Zagorje). The blue and yellow-green
hues symbolically reference water and the
natural surroundings of the spa.

DOBSON & ASSOCIATES

Studio: Bremmer & Goris Communications

Associative Color Response:
- mid-range green: classic
- dark blue: serene, credible, devoted

Color Scheme: near incongruous plus neutral with tinting

Adding white to the blue diminishes the intensity of the hue and fools the eye into believing that a pure gray color is included. Although only the transparency or volume of ink laid down in the halftone pattern has been manipulated, this method is an excellent way of creating a three-color design using only two inks. Different inks may yield highly unexpected results depending on the purity or build of the hue.

ENOUGH

Studio: Bremmer & Goris Communications

Associative Color Response:
- black: powerful, basic
- high-chroma yellow-orange: excitement, stimulating, fun

Color Scheme: near incongruous plus neutral

The three colors that make up this logotype have each been paired as a background and foreground color for two letters (black on red, red on yellow-orange, and yellow-orange on black). Stated in this order, it is easy to see the algorithmic pattern defined by the designer.

The overlap of colors, to create a depth of field in a narrow space, is one of the details that make this mark interesting.

INTELLIVUE UNPLUGGED

Designer/Art Director: Jun Li
Studio: Juno Studio

Associative Color Response:
- high-chroma red: brilliant, intense, energizing
- black: powerful, basic
- neutral gray: quality
- high-chroma yellow-green: new growth, sharp

Color Scheme: hue plus neutral tints

This logo for a wireless patient-monitoring system highlights the freedom and mobility patients gained from wireless technology through a disconnected circle that is projected in bright and cheery colors. The gray communicates a level of competency expected from the medical field, and the thickness of each stroke implies equality in the services provided. These colors build a complex picture of cutting-edge technology delivered with warmth and excitement.

HRT

Designer: Boris Ljubicic

Associative Color Response:
- high-chroma red: brilliant
- high-chroma blue: dignity
- neutral gray: quality

Color Scheme: two hues of a triad plus neutral tint

This logo reveals the acronym of the Croatian broadcasting corporation and includes a color representation of each arm—blue for television, red for radio, and white for joint services. The logo incorporates two red squares from the Croatian coat of arms that can be manipulated equally well on all static and motion collateral. This gives the designer ultimate control of the visual imagery while maintaining a consistent graphic standard.

THE DUB HOUSE

Designer: Kiley Del Valle
Creative Director: Jonathan Gouthier
Studio: Gouthier Design

Associative Color Response:
- pastel blue: pleasant, peaceful, happy
- neutral gray: quality
- black: powerful, basic

Color Scheme: one hue with neutrals (tinted)

The gray hue is used as a shadow to help build the mark dimension. The pastel blue is used to separate out the most meaningful part to help brand the mark long-term.

ENCODE

Designer: Holly Gressley
Interactive Designer: Doug Lloyd
Art Director: Petter Ringbom
Studio: Flat

Associative Color Response:
- high-chroma blue: dignified, lively, pleasant
- dark violet: power
- black: powerful

Color Scheme: incongruous

This incongruous color palette is made from two inks: blue (cyan) and red (magenta). These two inks are then overprinted to create a third additional color—black. This is an excellent way to stretch color on press to generate more hues than what is loaded in the inkwells.

SEN NEN BI

Designer: Hiroyuki Matsuishi

Associative Color Response:
- high-chroma blue: dignified, lively, pleasant
- high-chroma green: life, motion, growth
- high-chroma red: brilliant, intense, energizing

Color Scheme: direct complementary plus blue-violet

This logotype possesses one secondary and two primary hues. Visual consistency is brought about through the equal proportion of color application and font to create a dynamic mark.

TOMOPHASE

Designer/Art Director: Jun Li
Studio: Juno Studio

Associative Color Response:
- dark red: taste
- high-chroma blue: dignified
- black: powerful, basic

Color Scheme: incongruous plus neutral

Tomophase Corporation is a young high-tech company that specializes in developing innovative solutions for Minimally Invasive

Diagnostics (MID). This optical technology offers new ways of diagnosing diseases and performing operations. The Tomophase logo had to convey the innovation and technology of these novel optical devices, and their association with the medical field. Therefore, different shades of blue were used to connect the product to its working environment.

TOMOPHASE

Designer/Art Director: Jun Li
Studio: Juno Studio

Associative Color Response:
- high-chroma blue: dignified
- high-chroma blue-violet: charming
- black: powerful, basic

Color Scheme: simple analogous plus black

Prior studies for the Tomophase logo included the use of red with black or blue to draw attention to the first two syllables of the logo.

JAZZ LIFE

Designer: Hiroyuki Matsuishi

Associative Color Response:
- high-chroma red: brilliant, intense, energizing
- black: powerful, basic
- mid-range pink: restrained, soft, quiet

Color Scheme: one hue with tinting plus neutral

The Jazz Life logomark is an excellent example of effectively using a gradient to generate motion within a mark. The organic

typeface used within this design is partially layered (breaking out) on top of the red rectangle to also convey movement, and the free style of jazz.

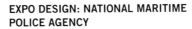

EXPO DESIGN: NATIONAL MARITIME POLICE AGENCY

Designer: Inyoung Choi

Associative Color Response:
- high-chroma red: brilliant, intense, energizing
- high-chroma blue: dignified, lively, pleasant
- high-chroma blue-violet: charming, elegant, refined

Color Scheme: incongruous with blue-violet

Designer Inyoung Choi uses a traditional color palette that is slightly off by adding an additional hue—blue-violet.

FOCUS FINANCE

Designer/Art Director: Jonathan Gouthier
Studio: Gouthier Design

Associative Color Response:
- high-chroma blue: dignified, lively, pleasant
- pastel blue: pleasant, peaceful, happy
- neutral gray: quality

Color Scheme: monochromatic plus neutral (tinted)

The pragmatic use of color within the focus logomark is superbly done. In this case, hue is implemented to create stress points and inflections within the mark.

COLLECTIBLE CREATIONS

Designer: Mark Raebel
Studio: Arsenal Design

Associative Color Response:
- gold: valuable, radiant
- high-chroma blue-green: new, pristine, pure
- pastel blue-green: mellow

Color Scheme: incongruous with tinting

The way in which the mark is cropped (square) in correspondence to the pragmatic color use creates a foreground, middle ground, and background. The typography is centered underneath the mark so the logo remains the focal point.

AEROBLOKS

Designer: Mark Raebel
Studio: Arsenal Design

Associative Color Response:
- high-chroma pink: exciting, stimulating, aggressive
- high-chroma violet: memories, power, import

Color Scheme: incongruous with overprinting

This incongruous color palette is made from two inks. A third color is created by overprinting the high-chroma pink (magenta) on top of the high-chroma blue (cyan).

EXPO DESIGN: HWACHEON-GUN

Designer: Inyoung Choi

Associative Color Response:
- high-chroma blue: dignified, lively, pleasant
- high-chroma orange: healing, growing, happy
- high-chroma yellow-green: new growth, sharp

Color Scheme: near split complementary with yellow-green

This highly unusual color palette is superbly executed. When trying to build unique color palettes, try using a traditional scheme that is slightly off. The uniqueness of the mark will be further helped by this approach.

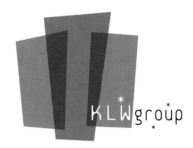

KLW GROUP

Designer: Mark Raebel
Studio: Arsenal Design

Associative Color Response:
- high-chroma red-violet: flamboyant, elegant
- neutral gray: quality
- mid-range red-violet: sensual, unique

Color Scheme: monochromatic with tinting

In this logo the hues are tinted and then overprinted to create additional hues.

The "*" marks placed around the typography, along with the overprinting and block shapes, help to generate kinetic energy.

VIA 101

Studio: AdamsMorioka

Associative Color Response:
- high-chroma yellow-green: new growth, sharp
- high-chroma red: brilliant, intense, energizing
- pastel blue: pleasant, peaceful, happy

Color Scheme: near split complementary

The simplicity of this mark coupled with the high-chroma hues creates a highly vivid logotype that is also stable. Again, a slightly off split complementary color palette is used to help create a unique color palette.

DR PALEY INC

Designer/Creative Director: Drew M. Dallet
Studio: Boom Creative

Associative Color Response:
- high-chroma blue: dignified, lively, pleasant
- neutral gray: quality
- black: powerful, basic

Color Scheme: one hue with neutrals (tinted)

The black hue in this logomark creates a third additional hue. This hue (neutral gray) is used to create a shadow for the blue mark as well as a visual tangent to connect the mark and typography. Conceptually, the neutral gray form references the MRIs and X-rays provided by Dr. Paley's services.

EXPO DESIGN: MINISTRY OF GOVERNMENT

Designer: Inyoung Choi

Associative Color Response:
- pastel blue: pleasant, peaceful, happy
- high-chroma blue-violet: charming, elegant, refined
- high-chroma yellow-green: sharp, new growth

Color Scheme: near incongruous with tinting

This incongruous color scheme is used superbly, helping to create a unique mark. A gross halftone screen pattern is added in pastel blue and yellow-green to help create kinetic energy.

CALIENTE MEXICAN RESTAURANT

Designer: Justina Wang

Associative Color Response:
- high-chroma green: life, motion, growth
- high-chroma red: brilliant, intense, energizing
- high-chroma orange: happy, healing, growing

Color Scheme: direct complementary with accent orange

When creating a dominant hue within the parent color scheme, using an accent color that is proportionately relative (the way in which the color is built) to the predominant hue will create a stress point or focal point.

EXPO DESIGN: KOREA-JAPAN SUPER EXPO

Designer: Inyoung Choi

Associative Color Response:
- dark red: elegant, refined, taste
- high-chroma blue: dignified, lively, pleasant
- high-chroma blue-violet: charming, elegant, refined

Color Scheme: near complementary

This double near complementary color palette helps to create a 3D illusion on a 2D plane. This is brought about through perspective and color gradients to make the "top" believable.

SMART ED

Designer/Creative Director: Drew M. Dallet
Studio: Boom Creative

Associative Color Response:
- black: powerful, basic
- high-chroma red-violet: flamboyant, elegant
- earth-tone yellow-orange: welcome, warm-hearted

Color Scheme: incongruous plus neutral

Within the parent color scheme—incongruous plus neutral—red-violet is used to unite the logomark. Warm colors come forth and cool colors recede, making the red-violet act as a catalyst within the mark.

THE TIPPERARY INN

Designer: Mark Raebel
Studio: Arsenal Design

Associative Color Response:
- black: powerful, basic
- high-chroma green: life, motion, growth
- neutral gray: quality

Color Scheme: one hue with neutrals (tinted)

The black and green hues in this logomark are symbolically used to reference Irish heritage and dark ale (Guinness). Additional content is added through pragmatic color use.

ST. PADDY'S DAY

Designer: Mark Raebel
Studio: Arsenal Design

Associative Color Response:
- dark yellow: flavorsome, active
- dark green: natural, growth, restful
- high-chroma green: life, motion, growth

Color Scheme: near simple analogous with shading

The signifiers embedded in this logomark are quite humorous. The "*" marks, tilted but full beer glass, three-leaf clover, and the use of two shades of green add up to one hell of a night!

THE JOE SKI CLUB

Designer/Creative Director: Drew M. Dallet
Studio: Boom Creative

Associative Color Response:
- dark green: natural, growth, restful
- high-chroma violet: memories, power, import
- black: powerful, basic

Color Scheme: incongruous plus neutral

The typography used for "The Joe Ski Clue" gives the mark dimension and depth.

Center *for* Justice, Tolerance, *and* Community
University of California, Santa Cruz

CENTER FOR JUSTICE, TOLERANCE, AND COMMUNITY, UNIVERSITY OF CALIFORNIA, SANTA CRUZ

Designer: Carol Chu

Associative Color Response:
- high-chroma blue-violet: charming, elegant, refined
- pastel blue-violet: elegant
- high-chroma blue: dignified, lively, pleasant
- pastel blue: pleasant, peaceful, happy

Color Scheme: simple analogous with tinting

The four blue bands in this logo represent justice, tolerance, community, and university. They are skillfully applied to create a 3D illusion and conceived in such a way as to give this mark unity and depth.

AMANGAH

Designer: Azin Ghazinia

Associative Color Response:
- black: powerful, basic
- high-chroma red: brilliant, intense, energizing
- high-chroma yellow-orange: excitement, stimulating, fun

Color Scheme: primary plus neutral

The economy of line found within this logotype is remarkable. The two letterforms, lowercase "a" and "g," not only act as initials for "amangah" but also operate as a face. The red and yellow dots reference human eyes, and the ascender and descender represent hair and the silhouette of a jaw line respectively.

THE TIPPERARY INN

Designer: Mark Raebel
Studio: Arsenal Design

Associative Color Response:
- pastel yellow-green: smooth, empathy, complete
- mid-range yellow-green: new growth
- high-chroma red: brilliant, intense, energizing

Color Scheme: near complementary with tinting

The two hues used within this mark are conveyed in a symbolic manner appropriate to the content. "A picture is worth a thousand words," as the old saying goes, and in this case the message is conveyed through the use of color.

THE DORRANCE GROUP

Designer: Mark Raebel
Studio: Arsenal Design

Associative Color Response:
- mid-range yellow-orange: comfortable
- mid-range blue-green: mellow
- neutral gray: quality

Color Scheme: incongruous plus neutral (tinted)

The Dorrance Group mark is constructed in a symmetrical manner. However, the mid-range yellow-orange and blue-green are added to energize the mark. The "dg" is tilted in an upward 45-degree angle, amplifying the positive kinetic energy found within this color scheme.

LET'S GO TO WORK

Designer: Mark Raebel
Studio: Arsenal Design

Associative Color Response:
- high-chroma yellow-orange: excitement, stimulating, fun
- pastel blue: pleasant, peaceful, happy
- high-chroma blue: dignified, lively, pleasant

Color Scheme: direct complementary with tinting

As shown here, a gross screen pattern and high-contrast image is best when it is used within a mark. In this way, the mark can be used in all media with no significant loss of quality.

CBP TV

Designer: Greg Friedrick

Associative Color Response:
- pastel blue: pleasant, peaceful, happy
- high-chroma blue: dignified, lively, pleasant
- high-chroma yellow-orange: excitement, stimulating, fun

Color Scheme: near complementary with tinting

The color scheme used in this logotype operates in a manner that clarifies how the acronym should be pronounced.

HAR-VEST

Designer/Creative Director: Drew M. Dallet
Studio: Boom Creative

Associative Color Response:
- high-chroma blue: dignified, lively, pleasant
- neutral gray: quality
- black: powerful, basic

Color Scheme: one hue with neutrals (tinted)

The black hue defines the silhouette of the mark, and is very legible from a distance. The high-chroma blue defines details within, while the neutral gray conveys highlights and softens the harshness of the mark.

DELTA CHI INTERNATIONAL CONVENTION

Designer/Creative Director: Drew M. Dallet
Studio: Boom Creative

Associative Color Response:
- black: powerful, basic
- high-chroma yellow-orange: excitement, stimulating, fun
- high-chroma red: brilliant, intense, energizing

Color Scheme: near incongruous plus neutral

The two warm, high-chroma hues are juxtaposed with the cool, bold black forms to create a mark that pops from within.

BUMBERSHOOT FORGE

Designer/Creative Director: Drew M. Dallet
Studio: Boom Creative

Associative Color Response:
- high-chroma yellow-orange: excitement, stimulating, fun
- high-chroma red-violet: flamboyant, elegant
- black: powerful, basic

Color Scheme: incongruous plus black

This beautifully executed color scheme harmonizes well with the script typeface, giving the mark a look of elegance.

DAVID ELLIS PHOTOGRAPHY

Designer/Creative Director: Drew M. Dallet
Studio: Boom Creative

Associative Color Response:
- neutral gray: quality
- dark gray: professional
- black: powerful, basic
- high-chroma red: brilliant, intense, energizing

Color Scheme: one hue with neutrals (tinted)

The method of separation is used in this logotype to pull out the most meaningful content. This is done through the use of color (red). Note that "photography," in red, is typeset much smaller than the rest of the mark. There are many technical ways to create separation (to mark out plainly the most meaningful part), and one of these is to be understated—this technique is superbly done here.

HUGHES HOLDINGS

Designer/Creative Director: Drew M. Dallet
Studio: Boom Creative

Associative Color Response:
- earth-tone red: good, warm-hearted, welcome
- dark blue: serene, credible, devoted
- white: clean, cool, innocent

Color Scheme: near incongruous with white

The white hue is achieved through type reversal. Many times an additional hue can be achieved by reversing out the type to the color of the substrate. However, if the paper is something other than white, the colors within the hue scheme will be tinted the hue of the substrate.

TIRESTORE.COM

Designer/Creative Director: Drew M. Dallet
Studio: Boom Creative

Associative Color Response:
- black: powerful, basic
- high-chroma red-violet: flamboyant, elegant
- high-chroma red-orange: friendly

Color Scheme: near simple analogous plus neutral

In this logomark, black is used to ground the mark while red-orange and red-violet are used to create a lively color combination that helps to create kinetic energy and make the mark memorable.

PRESCRIPTIONS PLUS

Designer/Creative Director: Drew M. Dallet
Studio: Boom Creative

Associative Color Response:
- high-chroma blue: service, clear, security
- high-chroma blue-green: new, pristine, pure
- black: powerful, basic

Color Scheme: simple analogous plus neutral

Choosing the right color scheme for the right job or subject matter can sometimes make a critical difference. In this case, designer Drew M. Dallet selected two hues that match the safety and health aspects concerning the delivery of prescription drugs.

VELO

Designer/Creative Director: Drew M. Dallet
Studio: Boom Creative

Associative Color Response:
- earth-tone red: good, welcome, warm-hearted
- high-chroma red-violet: flamboyant, elegant
- black: powerful, basic

Color Scheme: simple analogous plus neutral

This simple analogous color palette helps to convey the client's intent by creating a mark that appears to be both global and radiating out from the center. This is brought about through the use of warm and cool colors.

FIRST NATION SUPPLY

Designer/Creative Director: Drew M. Dallet
Studio: Boom Creative

Associative Color Response:
- high-chroma yellow-orange: excitement, stimulating, fun
- high-chroma red: brilliant, intense, energizing
- black: powerful, basic

Color Scheme: near incongruous plus neutral

The mark and color scheme for First National Supply borrows from a Native American symbol, Dreamcatcher, and reflects the owner's and client's cultural sensibilities.

IN SIGHT

Designer/Creative Director: Drew M. Dallet
Studio: Boom Creative

Associative Color Response:
- high-chroma blue-violet: charming, elegant, refined
- mid-range blue-violet: classic
- pastel blue-violet: elegant

Color Scheme: monochromatic with tinting

This simple monochromatic color study with tinting effectively creates movement from right to left. Emphasis is placed on "In" to create a stress point for proper pronunciation and inflection.

STATE OF QATAR:
THE PLANNING COUNCIL
AND THE GENERAL SECRETARIAT

Designer: Manar Al-Muftah

Associative Color Response:
- pastel yellow-orange: comfortable
- pastel blue: pleasant, peaceful, happy
- dark red: warm-hearted, welcome, good

Color Scheme: near triad

The color palette applied within these marks is both symbolic and indexical. The dark red/maroon hue is the state color, while pastel blue, and pastel yellow-orange reference the two halves of the landscape (the desert and the sky).

CHELSEA TITLE AGENCY

Designer/Creative Director: Drew M. Dallet
Studio: Boom Creative

Associative Color Response:
- gold: valuable, radiant
- black: powerful, basic
- high-chroma red: brilliant, intense, energizing

Color Scheme: near incongruous plus neutral

The Chelsea Title Agency crest is an excellent example of using the correct color combination to create a visual impression. In this case, gold, red, and black combine to help create a mark of prestige.

Note, when dealing with metallic inks, create a sidebar electronic mechanical that runs on the wastepaper surface of the printed job. Overprint the metallic inks, in different tints, with the other hues. Most printers, so long as there is no trim work, will print the sidebar with no additional cost. This will give you tremendous insight into how to use metallic inks more effectively and uniquely. This can be done with all hues.

CHABADUM JEWISH STUDENT CENTRAL

Designer: Marc Rabinowitz

Associative Color Response:
- high-chroma yellow-orange: excitement, stimulating, fun
- high-chroma yellow-green: sharp, new growth
- muddy gray: quality, basic

Color Scheme: near analogous using tertiary hues plus neutral (tinted)

The color combination used here creates a lively and energetic mark for the Jewish Student Central. Substitution is applied within the stroke of the "u" and "m" for recognition and cultural identity.

THE REBEL CONNECTION

Designer: Ken Kelleher

Associative Color Response:
- high-chroma red: brilliant, intense, energizing
- neutral gray: quality
- black: powerful, basic

Color Scheme: one hue with neutrals (tinted)

The red hue is used in a symbolic reference, whereas the swooping line work conceptually conveys the idea of connection.

MYOGENIX

Designer: James Sakamoto
Art Director: Mark Sackett
Studio: Sackett Design

Associative Color Response:
- high-chroma red: brilliant, intense, energizing
- high-chroma blue: dignified, lively, pleasant
- black: powerful, basic

Color Scheme: primary plus neutral

The two primary hues within this color palette are used to indicate the way in which "Myogenix" is pronounced.

SPORTY JOE CONSULTANCY

Studio: Plastic Soldier Factory Pte Ltd

Associative Color Response:
- neutral gray: quality
- high-chroma blue-green: new, pristine, pure
- high-chroma orange: happy, healing, growing

Color Scheme: near complementary plus neutral (tinted)

Substitution, warm and cool hues, and color value play an important role in the success of this mark. The blue-green hue harmonizes more appropriately with the neutral gray than the orange. (Both the blue-green and the neutral gray are cool colors and the eye makes an easier transition back and forth between these two components.) Orange is used as a shadow form and the human figure is placed in different positions to symbolize a multitude of sporting activities. All three hues have a near-same color value, thereby uniting the mark.

SOVA ARCHITECTURE

Studio: Hornall Anderson Design Works

Associative Color Response:
- high-chroma orange: happy, healing, growing
- neutral gray: quality
- dark gray: professional

Color Scheme: one hue with neutrals (tinted)

Separation is used to make a clear delineation between "Sova" and "Architecture." The "o" is further embellished to create a stress and focal point.

AX MILL

Designer: Tanya Ortega
Art Director: John T. Drew

Associative Color Response:
- high-chroma blue: dignified, lively, pleasant
- mid-range blue: pleasant, peaceful, happy
- high-chroma orange: happy, healing, growing

Color Scheme: direct complementary with tinting

Along with the form of the logomark, tinting is used to help create the illusion of a 3D logo on a 2D plane.

GLENSHORE

Designer: Nate Burgos

Associative Color Response:
- pastel blue: pleasant, peaceful, happy
- pastel green: classic
- mid-range green: classic

Color Scheme: near analogous with tinting

The combination of hues and form create a mark that looks very natural.

YUJIN ONO

Designer: Yujin Ono
Art Director: John T. Drew

Associative Color Response:
- black: powerful, basic
- mid-range blue-violet: classic
- high-chroma red: brilliant, intense, energizing

Color Scheme: near simple analogous plus neutral

The red hue is strategically placed to make the "Y" of Yujin pop. The mark is perfectly symmetrical, creating one centralized focal point, "Y."

YUJIN ONO

Designer: Yujin Ono
Art Director: John T. Drew

Associative Color Response:
- muddy gray: quality, basic
- neutral gray: quality
- dark gray: professional
- black: powerful, basic

Color Scheme: achromatic

An achromatic color palette is used here to create a mark that is conservative and professional. The two circles are added to help create a counterbalance and infuse the mark with a minimal amount of kinetic energy.

CURES NOW: FINDING CURES NOW FOR A BRIGHT FUTURE

Designer: Rendi Kusnadi Suzana

Associative Color Response:
- black: powerful, basic
- neutral gray: quality
- pastel blue-violet: peaceful, happy

Color Scheme: one hue with shading and tinting plus neutral

Note how the interlocking elements of the heart are woven in such a way that the mark becomes 2D. This helps to emphasize and unite the mark into a holistic symbol.

DAGGER

Designer: Manar Al-Muftah
Art Director: John T. Drew

Associative Color Response:
- high-chroma muddy orange: provoking
- mid-range muddy orange: inspiring
- pastel muddy orange: sound

Color Scheme: monochromatic with tinting

This dagger mark is beautifully executed. Substitution is applied within the handle of the dagger (Arabic typography that is part of the national anthem for the state of Qatar).

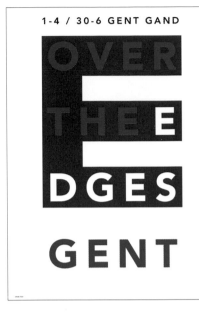

GENT GAND

Designer/Art Director: Ragna Hom
Studio: Thonik Design

Associative Color Response:
- high-chroma red: brilliant, intense, energizing
- high-chroma blue: dignified, lively, pleasant

Color Scheme: incongruous made from primaries plus neutral

Fracture, first described by Professor Ben Day of Virginia Commonwealth University, is an excellent visual technique to draw attention. In this case, this visual technique is used for a campaign of marks.

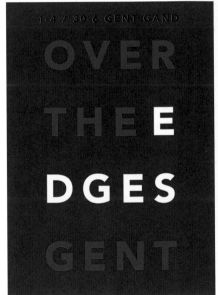

LESS + MORE

Designer/Art Director: Ragna Hom
Studio: Thonik Design

Associative Color Response:
- high-chroma red: brilliant, intense, energizing
- black: powerful, basic
- high-chroma blue: dignified, lively, pleasant

Color Scheme: incongruous made from primaries plus neutral

Fracture is used to help draw attention to the mark and create visual interest. (Fracture: to knock off the pre-existing plane content that is most relevant by rotating, flipping, chopping, cropping, and subtraction.)

ISLAND GENUINE SPORTS

Designer: Mark Raebel
Studio: Arsenal Design

Associative Color Response:
- high-chroma yellow-green: sharp, new growth,
- high-chroma blue-green: new, pristine, pure
- black: powerful, basic

Color Scheme: near simple analogous plus neutral

The Island Sports logomark is symmetrically balanced, creating a secure and stable composition. High-chroma yellow-green and blue-green are used to engender activity, making the mark more lively and appropriate to the content—an excellent color choice.

2005: THE YEAR OF THE ROOSTER

Designer: Chen Wang

Associative Color Response:
- mid-range yellow-orange: energetic, glow
- high-chroma red: brilliant, intense, energizing

Color Scheme: near incongruous plus neutral

This is an outstanding example of type as image. Red and black are used for their cultural significance within the Chinese-American community.

HOH

Designer: Nophadonh Phongsav
Art Director: John T. Drew

Associative Color Response:
- high-chroma blue: dignified, lively, pleasant
- high-chroma blue-violet: charming, elegant, refined
- mid-range yellow-green: new growth

Color Scheme: simple analogous plus dark yellow-green (tinted)

Gestalt is used most effectively in the HOH logotype. Note how the form/counterform relationships are brought about through economy of line.

NTH DEGREE CONSULTING

Designers: Clifford Boobyer and Andrew Philip
Studio: Firedog Design

Associative Color Response:
- high-chroma yellow-orange: excitement, stimulating, fun
- pastel yellow-orange: comfortable
- black: powerful, basic

Color Scheme: monochromatic with tinting plus neutral

The tinting and gradients applied within this logotype help to create a 3D illusion so that "Nth°" floats forward.

THRILLZ

Designer: Tarun Deep Girdher

Associative Color Response:
- high-chroma red-orange: energizing
- high-chroma yellow-orange: excitement, stimulating, fun
- high-chroma blue: dignified, lively, pleasant

Color Scheme: split complementary

A highly active color scheme coupled with exhilarating line work creates an exciting and energetic mark. Note how the line work used for this mark harmonizes with the color scheme chosen.

AQUALUNG

Designer: Savio Alphonso

Associative Color Response:
- high-chroma blue-violet: charming, elegant, refined
- high-chroma blue: dignified, lively, pleasant
- pastel blue: pleasant, peaceful, happy

Color Scheme: simple analogous with tinting

The aqualung mark is an excellent example of a simple analogous color scheme. Designer Savio Alphonso creates a third additional hue by tinting the high-chroma blue-violet to denote imperfection within the lungs.

CENTRAAL MUSEUM

Designer/Art Director: Ragna Hom
Studio: Thonik Design

Associative Color Response:
- high-chroma orange: healing, growing, happy
- white: clean, cool, innocent
- black: powerful, basic

Color Scheme: one hue with neutral and white

Once again, the lowercase "c" for the Centraal Museum is incorporated into the design to create a mark that will appeal to young and old alike.

CENTRAAL MUSEUM

Designer/Art Director: Ragna Hom
Studio: Thonik Design

Associative Color Response:
- black: powerful, basic
- high-chroma red: brilliant, intense, energizing
- high-chroma green: life, motion, growth

Color Scheme: direct complementary plus neutral

The high-chroma, direct complementary color palette used for the Centraal Museum is an excellent color choice to attract kids of any age. The "c" of the Centraal Museum is used throughout the campaign to create brand recognition—an excellent example of substitution.

CENTRAAL KIDDS

Designer/Art Director: Ragna Hom
Studio: Thonik Design

Associative Color Response:
- black: powerful, basic
- high-chroma red: brilliant, intense, energizing
- high-chroma green: life, motion, growth

Color Scheme: direct complementary plus neutral

The high-chroma, direct complementary color palette used for the Centraal Museum is an excellent color choice to attract kids of any age. The "c" of the main Centraal Museum logo is used throughout the campaign to create brand recognition—an excellent example of substitution.

HE THE BEST EVAN OF WIM T. SCHIPPERS

Designer/Art Director: Ragna Hom
Studio: Thonik Design

Associative Color Response:
- high-chroma red: brilliant, intense, energizing
- high-chroma green: life, motion, growth
- black: powerful, basic

Color Scheme: direct complementary plus neutral

Separation is applied in order to help speed up recognition and to create visual interest.

MIRACLE REACH

Designer: Brenda Spivack
Studio: Red Table

Associative Color Response:
- high-chroma yellow-green: sharp, new growth
- high-chroma blue: dignified, lively, pleasant
- neutral gray: quality

Color Scheme: near incongruous plus neutral (tinted)

The high-chroma blue and high-chroma yellow-green is realized in such a way as to create a halo affect—most appropriate for the content.

ABSECON

Designer: Scott W. Santoro
Studio: Worksight

Associative Color Response:
- golden yellow: dignified
- black: powerful, basic
- pastel green: classic

Color Scheme: near analogous with tinting plus neutral

Repetition is used within the absecon mark to create continuity and activity. A golden-yellow and pastel green are toned back to create a thoughtful visual hierarchy within a complex mark.

HEART BRA

Studio: Essex Two

Associative Color Response:
- high-chroma pink: exciting, stimulating, aggressive
- pastel pink: soft, sweet, tender, comfortable
- mid-range pink: restrained, soft, quiet

Color Scheme: monochromatic with tinting

If used inappropriately, culturally identifiable symbols can become trite quickly. In this case, repetition of form and color tinting are applied so that the mark takes on a more unique shape.

NEVEROUS CONSTRUCTION

Studio: Essex Two

Associative Color Response:
- black: powerful, basic
- muddy gray: quality, basic
- neutral gray: quality

Color Scheme: achromatic

The Neverous Construction logo was created for a building contractor. In this case, the 3D shape of the mark and the overall mass conceptually relate to the subject matter. An achromatic color palette is applied to make the mark appear even more massive.

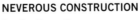

RONALD MCDONALD CHILDREN'S CHARITIES

Studio: Essex Two

Associative Color Response:

- high-chroma yellow: agreeable, pleasant, welcome, youthful
- high-chroma red: brilliant, intense, energizing
- black: powerful, basic

Color Scheme: incongruous plus neutral

The Ronald McDonald Children's Charities mark is an excellent example of empathy carried out through the execution of form and pragmatic color use.

SAGENT

Designer: Brenda Spivack
Studio: Red Table

Associative Color Response:

- high-chroma orange: healing, growing, happy
- mid-range orange: gentle, enticing, good spirit
- high-chroma yellow-orange: excitement, stimulating, fun
- high-chroma yellow-green: sharp, new growth
- mid-range yellow-green: new growth
- pastel yellow-green: smooth

Color Scheme: simple analogous

In both marks, color gradients are used to help create kinetic movement. To further create activity within the mark the logo is placed at an angle, and white activity lines (reversed out) are incorporated to allow the viewing audience to move freely in and out of the mark.

STATE OF MIND GALLERY

Designer: April Medina

Associative Color Response:

- black: powerful, basic
- high-chroma orange: healing, growing, happy
- high-chroma yellow-green: sharp, new growth

Color Scheme: near incongruous plus neutral with tinting

The physicality of form and pragmatic color use create a composition that reflects the state of mind of the gallery.

SOMMESE DESIGN

Designers: Kristin Sommese
and Lanny Sommese
Studio: Sommese Design

Associative Color Response:
- mid-range yellow-green: new growth
- mid-range pink: restrained, soft, quiet
- black: powerful, basic

Color Scheme: near complementary
plus neutral

The mark was created for Sommese Design,
a graphic design studio where the two principals
are a husband-and-wife team. This logo is
a wonderful example of representing this
design studio. Note that the mark is made
up of signifiers that denote both male and
female, including color.

ZONE DEFENSE

Studio: Essex Two

Associative Color Response:
- black: powerful, basic
- high-chroma blue: dignified, lively, pleasant
- high-chroma red: brilliant, intense,
  energizing

Color Scheme: primary plus neutral

This modular-system mark symbolizes
a collaboration of several communication
firms. The two primary hues, red and blue,
together with black are used to denote
this collaboration.

360° LIVING

Designer/Art Director: David Ferrell
Studio: HMA

Associative Color Response:
- dark green: natural, growth, restful
- high-chroma blue-green: new, pristine, pure
- high-chroma yellow-green: sharp,
  new growth

Color Scheme: analogous with shading

The combination of a color scheme applied
and the shapes and line work found within
the mark create a highly energetic logo that
conceptually fits the content.

3W

Designer: Steven Gonsowski
Art Director: John T. Drew

Associative Color Response:
- muddy gray: quality, basic
- high-chroma orange: healing,
  growing, happy
- high-chroma blue-violet: charming,
  elegant, refined

Color Scheme: near complementary plus muddy neutral (tinted)

The high-chroma orange and blue-violet create a masterfully energetic logotype. The muddy gray is used to tone down the mark and give it a more professional feel. Note in this case that background color studies were created (for example, muddy gray), to determine choice of paper.

IDENTITY: THE BRANDING SPECIALISTS

Designer: Steve Gonsowski
Art Director: John T. Drew

Associative Color Response:
- high-chroma blue: dignified, lively, pleasant
- high-chroma orange: healing,
  growing, happy
- black: powerful, basic

Color Scheme: direct complementary plus neutral

The use of a thumbprint to form the "d" in "Identity" suggests a human touch to the company's workings.

QATAR

Designer: Tarek Atrissi

Associative Color Response:
- high-chroma blue-green: new, pristine, pure
- high-chroma orange: healing,
  growing, happy
- high-chroma red: brilliant, intense,
  energizing

Color Scheme: split complementary

This wonderfully elegant mark is beautifully executed both in the physicality of form and in the color palette applied.

Four Colors

The globalization of printing, coupled with interactive and motion design, has meant that the cost of adding colors to a logo is no longer prohibitive. Corporations are no longer restricted to a limited color palette for their mark. However, this can make designing logos more complex and harder to control. Today we are not only faced with understanding print production, we are also charged with understanding the Web, its interactivity, motion design, and, in many cases, environmental graphic design, packaging, textiles, and product design. Managing color has never been so complex, both in its technical application and its conceptual direction. In this chapter, some of the world's most inspiring four-color logomarks are showcased to help us understand how these issues have been addressed by using hue to its full potential.

From large corporations to small fashion houses, from building facilities to advertising, marks and their colorful use engulf our environment and influence our consumption. Understanding how, when, and why colors should be used in a given circumstance is the mainstay of hue application.

TEAM CDLS

Designer: Laurie Churchman
Studio: Designiore

Associative Color Response:
- mid-orange: good spirits, inviting
- high-chroma blue: dignity, pleasing
- red: surging, brilliant
- green: new growth, hope

Color Scheme: split complementaries plus one hue (tetrad)

This logomark uses a tetrad color arrangement (a contrast of four or more colors on the color wheel) for emphasis. The equally weighted blue, green, and negative white line encompass the colors and create unity in the design.

S. P. SHAUGHNESSEY & COMPANY

Designer/Art Director: Drew M. Dallet
Studio: Boom Creative

Associative Color Response:
- green: brimming with life, thinking
- gray: quality, practical
- black: strong, prestigious

Color Scheme: monochromatic plus neutral (tinted)

The equal line weight of the inverted white type creates a "C" and "P" individually and a broken "S" as a whole. In addition, the counterform defines a contiguous green "S" that is unified with the white stroke through proportion. The white stroke is half the weight of the green stroke.

CAMPUS LASIK

Designer/Art Director: Drew M. Dallet
Studio: Boom Creative

Associative Color Response:
- green: clear, thinking
- gray: quality, practical
- blue: service, professional
- black: school, prestigious

Color Scheme: analogous plus neutral (tinted)

The font choice connotes a university emblem, while the thick-and-thin line quality unifies the mark in a way similar to the stitching used to attach a badge to a college leather jacket. The blue fields seem to indicate the circular form of the iris.

Ask Me! About UNLV

Designer: Ken Kelleher

Associative Color Response:
- orange: cheerful, warm
- gray: passion, practical
- black: school, prestigious
- red: brilliant, extrovert

Color Scheme: two hues plus achromatic tints

The sans-serif type adds to the quick read, and the orange exclamation point emphasizes the passion and energy with which questions will be answered. Hierarchy in the statement is determined by the tints and hues of each word, with "about" being the least important. The change from sans serif to serif in addition to the red color emphasizes "UNLV."

FIREDOG

Designers: Clifford Boobyer and Andrew Philip
Studio: Firedog Design

Associative Color Response:
• red: dynamic, provocative
• gray: professional, solid
• black: powerful, basic

Color Scheme: one hue with tinting
and shading

The subtle shift from shadow to highlight creates dimensionality to the button. Although the dog sits on a narrow depth of field, adding black to the red prevents the tint from turning pink and reinforces the dog's vigor.

WEB•X INTERNET SOLUTIONS

Designer/Art Director: Drew M. Dallet
Studio: Boom Creative

Associative Color Response:
• red: dynamic, provocative
• gray: professional, solid
• black: strong, invulnerable

Color Scheme: one hue plus achromatic tints

The white "x" seems to radiate out from the red dot at the center of the logomark. This is enhanced by the smooth transition from thick to thin line, the elliptical gray shapes in the background, and subtle simultaneous contrast of the gray and red triangles. These qualities are mirrored in the type choice and placement.

TECH SOURCE SOLUTIONS

Designer/Art Director: Drew M. Dallet
Studio: Boom Creative

Associative Color Response:
• dark red: develop, experience
• green: versatility, trustworthy
• black: basic, invulnerable

Color Scheme: complementary tints
plus neutral

The shadow produced by the gear belies the flat appearance of the wheel. The lack of dimension is created through the equal line weights and shades of complementary color (red and green), while the tint of black in the shadow defines depth.

ST. PATRICK'S MASSACRE

Designer: Mark Raebel
Studio: Arsenal Design

Associative Color Response:
• green: St. Patrick's Day, springtime
• high-chroma green-yellow: fruity, new growth
• yellow: wheat, cheerful
• black: basic, neutral

Color Scheme: analogous plus neutral

Overlapping of imagery communicates depth, and in this logomark creates the illusion that the knife is spearing the shamrock. Yellow is used in both the foreground of the knife and the background field. This helps to unify the composition but does not detract from the implied depth.

SAINT PAT'S AT THE TIP

Designer: Mark Raebel
Studio: Arsenal Design

Associative Color Response:
- green: St. Patrick's Day, refreshing
- orange: tasty, friendly
- black: heavy, basic

Color Scheme: two points of a triad with tinting plus neutral

The orange calls attention to the predominant hierarchy and helps to slow the reader's eye, which is essential for this typeface. In addition, the bold white line around the distressed black type helps to clarify the readability and unifies "Saint Pat's" with the secondary type.

PEDIATRIC PALLIATIVE CARE

Studio: Essex Two

Associative Color Response:
- red: stimulating, fun
- blue: happy, pleasing
- yellow: energetic, warmth
- black: school, spatial

Color Scheme: additive primaries plus neutral

Not only are the primary colors equally spaced from each other on the color wheel, they are also equally spaced within this logomark. This helps to reinforce the building-block effect of the interlinking structure without diminishing the significance of the mark as too childish.

SPOTLIGHT PROJECTS

Studio: Essex Two

Associative Color Response:
- yellow: anticipation, welcome
- black: spatial, mysterious

Color Scheme: one hue plus neutral with tints and shades

The subtlety with which the spotlights are trained is achieved through the definition of each tint. This effect can only be accomplished through controlled overprinting of one gradation over another and a precise halftone dot that gradually reveals the foreground of the stage.

MICROSOFT OFFICE LICENSING PRODUCTS.COM

Designer: Ann M. Simon

Associative Color Response:
- orange: producing, vital
- blue: strength, work
- green: use, hope
- yellow: active, vital

Color Scheme: complementary (orange, blue) plus diad (yellow, green)

The shift from equally weighted sans-serif typefaces in the background to a serif typeface in the foreground increases the depth in this narrow field. The thick and thin stroke of the "O" calls attention to the triangles created within the blue field.

ETERNAL HEALTH & WELLNESS

Designer: Carlo Irigoyen
Art Director: Brenda Spivack
Studio: Red Table

Associative Color Response:
• yellow-orange: luxuriance, energy
• brown: life, warm

Color Scheme: two hues with tints

The equal line weight of the mark is in stark contrast to the thick and thin strokes of the typography. The juxtaposition of contrasting line weight allows both the logomark and the logotype to work independently of each other. Together the logo is unified through the binary opposition as yin/yang and the commonality of the color.

GRACHTEN FESTIVAL

Designer/Art Director: Ragna Hom
Studio: Thonik Design

Associative Color Response:
• red: brilliant, dynamic
• blue: spaciousness, upward
• purple: thought, atmospheric

Color Scheme: three hues plus tints and neutralizing

The soft tints of blue give an airy quality to this mark, making the thick red type appear as if it is floating on the blue background. This counterintuitive approach works well— even where the background violates the red type, the readability is uncompromised.

URBAN VISIONS

Studio: Hornall Anderson Design Works

Associative Color Response:
• high-chroma blue: classy, reposed
• blue-green: pristine, tranquillity
• high-chroma yellow-green: biology, strength
• high-chroma green-yellow: lemony, new growth

Color Scheme: near complex analogous

The analogous color scheme unifies the logomark so completely that upon initial viewing it is easy to notice only the footprint and overlook the leaf and water droplet. To complete the synchronization of elements throughout the logomark and logotype, the water droplet is used in substitution for the dot on the letter "i."

FULLERTON ARBORETUM

Designer: Jay Pilar
Art Director: John Drew

Associative Color Response:
• orange: healing, growing
• yellow: welcome, noble
• black: neutral, life

Color Scheme: analogous tints plus neutral

The layered hands are an excellent example of metaphor. In substitution of a flower, they clearly communicate the stewardship of an arboretum.

ESOY

Studio: Sommese Design
Designer: Lanny Sommese

Associative Color Response:
- yellow: youthful, energy
- red-orange: healing, tasty
- blue-green: pristine, consistent
- black: powerful, life

Color Scheme: direct complementary with tinting and accent hue plus neutral

This logotype for an online distributor of soy-based products is crisp and bright. The designer used a color palette that would be in keeping with the perception of soy as a healthy product. The short name and vibrant colors create an easily identifiable and memorable logotype.

MARTA HERFORD: PARKKARTE

Designer/Art Director: Ragna Hom
Studio: Thonik Design

Associative Color Response:
- cyan: pleasing, unique
- magenta: exciting, promising
- gray: quality, passion
- black: noble, expensive

Color Scheme: subtractive primaries plus neutral with tinting

This logo and identity system for a museum designed by world-renowned architect Frank Gehry in Herford, Germany, consists of three stripes of color used in multiple combinations with a standardized black logotype stating

"MARTa Herford." The stripes are used to develop a display face that adapts depending upon the situation and yet references each department within the museum: design, art, and architecture. In this case, color is used to communicate remarkable diversity with precision.

LAGUNA BEACH DOG PARK

Designer: Tricia Diaz
Studio: Cherrybomb

Associative Color Response:
- blue: vibrant, summer
- green: grass, life

Color Scheme: simple near analogous with tints

The setting of the park among the hills is established in the green background tints and also serves as a metaphorical reference to the love that owners feel toward their pets. Also, this heart shape is subtly referenced in the sitting position of the dog and literally revealed in the dog's tags.

REVALESIO

Studio: Hornall Anderson Design Works

Associative Color Response:
- blue: cool, relaxed
- yellow-green: strength, sunlight
- blue-green: pristine, consistent
- black: life, strong

Color Scheme: near analogous plus neutral

Overprinting the high-chroma yellow-green and the pure blue results in a saturated blue-green. A painterly quality is revealed by

the imprecise fit of the color mixture to the black outline. This helps to bring a hand-crafted feel to the logo that implies a loving and one-on-one attention. If the type did not reinforce the concept through a hand-drawn logotype, the concept would be negated.

ADVENTURE TRAVEL GROUP

Designer/Art Director: Saied Farisi

Associative Color Response:
• green: life, motion

Color Scheme: monochromatic tints

The sharp points of the logomark reference many things. Most obvious is the reference to a tree, but, like a needle on a compass, the tangents also indicate that there are many paths to take. Referencing words in the dictionary also provides insight for the designer. Among the many words listed are "promontory," "spit," and "bluff."

ISLAND SPORTS

Designer: Mark Raebel
Studio: Arsenal Design

Associative Color Response:
• blue: sky, wet
• yellow-green: sunlight, trendy
• yellow: pleasant, vigorous
• yellow-orange: fun, exciting

Color Scheme: near complementary with analogous

The stroke weight of the typeface is the base proportion of the entire logomark and helps to create unity. For example, the thickness of each orange, yellow, and green stripe is 3 times the thickness of the font. The space between each stripe is 1.5 times the thickness, and the blue border is 5 times the thickness. This use of prime number proportionality (1, 3, 5, 7) can be seen throughout the mark and is a common method of creating intuitively pleasing compositions.

NATIONAL RESEARCH INSTITUTE OF CULTURAL PROPERTIES

Designer: Inyoung Choi

Associative Color Response:
• blue: dignity, unique
• yellow-green: strength, sharp
• brown: folksy, sheltering

Color Scheme: two points of a tetra plus neutral tinting

The horizon line created by the overlapping fields of green and blue attract the eye and create a perception of depth. However, a psychological shift in color takes place as the brain tries to make sense of the white field. According to atmospheric conditions, light colors come forward and dark colors recede. In this composition, interest is held by the inverse of that principle. Where the mind believes depth will occur, a light color (white) is placed.

ADRIA RESORTS

Creative/Art Directors: Davor Bruketa and Nikola Zinic

Associative Color Response:
• blue: water, sky
• black: basic, elegant

Color Scheme: monochromatic plus neutral

This logomark for a consortium of resorts along Croatia's coast accurately depicts the brilliant color and light of the area. The overlapping circles communicate unity and the nature of the water to change the appearance of form through reflection.

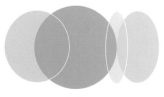

BEFU EYE CLINIC

Designer: Hiroyuki Matsuishi

Associative Color Response:
• orange: healing, whimsical
• blue: service, security

Color Scheme: direct complementary with tinting

The counterforms of the type create a dynamic composition as the mind's eye switches from foreground to background to create the bird or read the name of the company. For example, the wing and eye of the bird create the counters of the "B." In contrast, the overlapping of the "e" and "f" switch from letterform to foot and leg respectively. By lessening the recognition of the letterforms as the word progresses, the designer is able to keep the audience's interest by forcing them to solve the puzzle.

ATTENEX

Studio: Hornall Anderson Design Works

Associative Color Response:
• blue: spaciousness, levels

Color Scheme: monochromatic plus neutral

This logo seems to undulate in space like a cloud in the sky. The soft overlaying of color, the tilt of the letterforms, and the shift in size create a boiling effect that attracts the viewer's attention to the logotype.

SEED (SUSTAINABLE ENERGY EFFICIENT DESIGN)

Illustrator/Art Director: Scott A. Gunderson

Associative Color Response:
• earth-tone red-brown: sheltering, durable
• pastel green: calm, natural
• black: spatial, invulnerable

Color Scheme: complementary tints/shades plus neutral

Traditionally, red and green are signifiers for Christmas. This color association can be negated through the tints and shades of each hue as well as a disproportionate usage of one color over another. The designer has used these techniques to emphasize the development and construction of energy-efficient homes.

GLENSHORE

Designer: Nate Burgos
Studio: Nate Burgos, Inc.

Associative Color Response:
• blue: spacious, security
• green: foliage, lakes
• black: expensive, prestigious

Color Scheme: near analogous tints plus neutral

Blue is the common hue running through the background and leaf pattern that represents the shore and unifies the composition. The syllabification of the type through placement on the background acknowledges the color selection without being overt.

IRELAND

Designer: Mark Raebel
Studio: Arsenal Design

Associative Color Response:
• green: Irish, brimming with life

Color Scheme: analogous with tinting

The two overlapping green tints produce a more pure color. This is a result of increased saturation as the white is eliminated from the hue. This can often be a negative effect when trapping two pastel colors around type or image. However, this logomark uses the effect in a positive way to generate a green that is near, but not the same as, the outline of the shamrock.

PLASTIC SOLDIER FACTORY

Studio: Plastic Soldier Factory

Associative Color Response:
• gray: passion, professional
• black: spatial, strong

Color Scheme: achromatic

This logomark has excellent depth achieved through minute variation in value. Multiple colors and fields can be implied through a commanding usage of tints and shades. The layers build to create an acronym that is revealed when the full name is placed on the uppermost plane. The equally spaced letters of the full name create a horizontal alignment that runs strictly perpendicular to the crossbar in the "F" of the acronym.

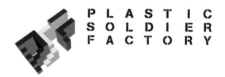

UPSHOT

Designer: Nicolas Ammann
Studio: 86 The Onions

Associative Color Response:
• cyan: energetic, happy
• high-chroma pink: stimulating, high-energy
• black: powerful, strong
• gray: enduring, solid
• brown: delicious, rich

Color Scheme: monochromatic plus neutral

The colors of this concentrated energy drink reflect its flavors, while the inverted arrow implies how quickly the drink should be consumed and will take effect. The type choice in combination with the color allows the packaging to look at home in a gas station or a hip club.

Five Colors

Most, if not all five-color marks are created with four inks or fewer—not many logos are created with five spot hues. With the globalization of printing and the Internet, many companies are now opting for multicolored logomarks, which was unheard of just a decade ago. Corporations and small businesses that use the Internet, multimedia, broadcast television, and/or motion graphics to advertise and sell their goods and services are becoming more aware of the impact that color has on their patrons. With the low cost and high quality of personal printers, many businesses, large and small, can now print in-house on demand with no significant loss of quality. This is truly a color revolution that equalizes the budgetary playing field of large and small businesses.

With that said, understanding color theory—including subtractive, additive, and 3D design—and having a knowledge of empirically tested color schemes, will improve the quality of color use within the marketplace dramatically. Just because a mark has multiple color use does not mean it is good. In fact, the chances of a mark being perceived as out-of-kilter increases as complexity increases. Even the best five-color marks demonstrate a level of constraint.

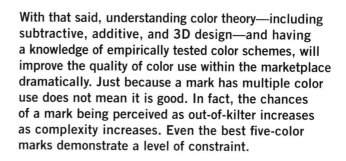

STORYTELLER: DIANE MACKLIN

Studio: Conceptual Geniuses

Associative Color Response:
- dark orange: exhilarating, provoking
- high-chroma orange: warm, communication

Color Scheme: complex analogous with tinting and shading

This five-color logomark, including tints and shades, is an excellent example of successfully limiting the range of hues to keep the mark intact. In doing so, the squiggly lines, stars, sun, heart, human figure, and bird (representing thought) easily become one with the human face and typography. Most successful marks having this number of hues limit the palette in some way to harmonize the mark. In this case, the palette is a complex analogous color scheme.

INTERNATIONAL CRICKET COUNCIL

Studio: Minale Bryce Design Strategy

Associative Color Response:
- high-chroma green: motion
- high-chroma blue: lively, upward
- high-chroma red: intense, energizing
- black: powerful

Color Scheme: near split complementary with tinting plus neutral

Control and restraint is applied in this color scheme to create a superbly executed mark. A near split complementary plus black is used in an effective manner. The red dot, used as an accent color in the word "Cricket," is just large enough so that the viewer's eye is pulled down into the typography. The black typography acts as a ground and is flat. This allows the earthlike ball to explode three-dimensionally off the page. Tinting is used to help create this 3D illusion.

ISLAND SPORTS

Designer: Mark Raebel
Studio: Arsenal Design

Associative Color Response:
- neutral gray: quality
- pastel green: trustworthy
- pastel yellow-green: pleasant
- pastel of dark yellow-orange: exhilarating
- pastel earth-tone orange: welcome

Color Scheme: near complex analogous with tinting and shading

This near complex analogous color scheme uses both tinting and shading to control the value and harmonize the mark. This allows all five components of the logo to act as one.

YOTIN FOUNDATION

Designer: Triesta Hall
Studio: Blu Art & Design

Associative Color Response:
- burgundy: elegant
- high-chroma yellow-orange: energy, enterprise
- high-chroma blue-violet: dignity, lively
- high-chroma violet: important
- pastel blue-violet: classic, powerful

Color Scheme: direct/near complementary with tinting plus a burgundy accent

A disproportionate use of color (blue-violet) unites the Yotin Foundation logotype and at the same time constrains the color scheme. The other four hues are used as accent colors to create an upbeat color palette.

ISTRAGRAFIKA

Creative/Art Directors: Davor Bruketa
and Nikola Zinic

Associative Color Response:
- high-chroma blue: lively
- dark orange: exhilarating
- high-chroma orange: happy
- high-chroma green: lively, motion
- high-chroma red: brilliant, exhilarating

Color Scheme: complex tetrad

The istragrafika logomark uses numerous color techniques to create an extremely interesting mark. So that the high-chroma blue and orange do not create simultaneous contrast and create a clashing of color, the dark orange is placed in between to harmonize the two hues. The orange is neutralized by adding a percentage of blue to create the dark orange. The orange and red are left intact and juxtaposed with the green to create pronounced simultaneous contrast. Using a small proportion of hue as an accent, in comparison to the blue field, pronounced simultaneous contrast is induced, creating a lively interplay within the complex tetrad.

SALES

Designer: Chihiro Katoh

Associative Color Response:
- white: innocent
- black: powerful, school
- high-chroma yellow-orange: joy
- dark orange: exhilarating
- high-chroma orange: childlike

Color Scheme: simple analogous with shading plus black and white

To control the complexity of this mark, a simple analogous color palette is used. The color palette chosen harmonizes well with the childlike illustration. The hues of black and white are used to give the mark depth, as well as a major focal point that pops.

RODAN + FIELDS DERMATOLOGISTS

Designer: Chihiro Katoh

Associative Color Response:
- high-chroma yellow-orange: healthy, pleasant
- black: powerful
- high-chroma yellow-green: strength
- dark green: trustworthy
- high-chroma blue: vibrant

Color Scheme: random—using one primary, one secondary, and two tertiary hues

It is important when using a random color palette to constrain the outcome in some formal manner. In this case, scale (primarily) and the consistency of form is used to constrain the color scheme so that it does not look chaotic.

ANEMONE

Designer: Mark Raebel
Studio: Arsenal Design

Associative Color Response:
- pastel mid-range orange: good spirits
- pastel mid-range red-violet: elegant, charming
- pastel pink: comfortable
- pastel of red-orange: friendly

Color Scheme: complex analogous with tinting and shading

The color value of the mark is controlled through tinting and shading to harmonize it into a cohesive whole. In addition to the typeface chosen, the complex analogous color palette limits the intricacy of hues and harmonizes the mark.

THE TIPPERARY INN

Designer: Mark Raebel
Studio: Arsenal Design

Associative Color Response:
• black: powerful, elegant
• high-chroma orange: tasty
• mid-range orange: inviting
• high-chroma green: Irish

Color Scheme: two points of a tetrad with tinting plus black

Constraining the color palette helps to simplify the complexity of the logomark, and at the same time creates a color palette that is uniquely suited for the content. The high-chroma orange is tinted to create three distinct hues that are used to create the 3D effect found in "The Tip."

AUTUMN TECHNOLOGY

Studio: Bremmer & Goris Communications

Associative Color Response:
• high-chroma blue-violet: powerful, elegant
• high-chroma orange: growing, communication
• mid-range orange: inviting
• dark orange: stimulating, provoking

Color Scheme: near complementary with tinting

This two-spot color logomark possesses five hues through the use of tinting—a superb example of stretching the color palette (with no additional cost to the client) to create greater intrigue. Note how all the leaves are uniformed (modular) and are rotated to create the mark.

ENVIRO PRO

Designer: Irene Marx
Studio: a+morph

Associative Color Response:
• black: powerful, elegant
• neutral gray: quality
• dark orange: exhilarating, inspiring
• high-chroma blue: wet
• high-chroma green: springtime, wilderness

Color Scheme: two points of a split complementary with an accent plus neutral with tinting

This complex color palette helps to create a wonderful mark that represents the environment we live in. The color palette is divided into two halves: green and blue are used to represent the earth, and black, gray, and orange-brown are used to denote humans. The three figures are holding hands to create the earth—an excellent color strategy that helps to reveal the overall concept.

NICK JR

Studio: AdamsMorioka

Associative Color Response:
• high-chroma orange: growing, happy
• mid-range orange: sweet, inviting
• dark orange: stimulating
• high-chroma blue: thought-provoking
• dark blue: service

Color Scheme: direct complementary with tinting and neutralizing

In the Nick Jr marks, the color technique of neutralizing is used to create multiple hues. Neutralizing occurs when black—or, in this case, its complementary color—is used to create additional hues. This would also be considered overprinting.

WORLD OF WATER

Designer: Erin Wright

Associative Color Response:
- muddy gray: quality, classic
- high-chroma blue: wet
- pastel blue-green: new
- mid-range blue-green: liquid
- high-chroma blue-green: ocean

Color Scheme: simple analogous with tinting, shading, and overprinting

The continents found within the logomark use a combination of tinting, shading, and overprinting. The tinting is to add white with the aid of a screened percentage. In this case, blue and blue-green are added together at 100% of color with a percentage of black to create the dark hues found within the mark.

ENCLAVE AT SUNRISE

Designer/Art Director: Erik Chrestensen
Studio: Chrestensen Designworks

Associative Color Response:
- earth-tone red: warm-hearted, wholesome
- high-chroma orange: healing, warm
- mid-range yellow-orange: inviting
- mid-range orange: gentle
- high-chroma yellow-orange: stimulating

Color Scheme: simple analogous with tinting and shading

This simplistic color palette is an excellent associative match for the subject matter. Elegant in its approach, the symmetrical execution befits a sunrise.

TRE VIDA

Designer: Celeste Parrish

Associative Color Response:
- pastel blue: pleasant, refreshing
- high-chroma yellow-green: strength
- mid-range pink: sentimental
- high-chroma orange: inviting
- dark red: elegant, refined

Color Scheme: near tetrad with tinting

The harmony of high-chroma colors coupled with consistency of typeface chosen creates a logotype that is both lively and inviting.

DISCOVERY DAY CARE

Studio: Essex Two

Associative Color Response:
- black: basic
- high-chroma blue: lively, happy
- high-chroma red: stimulating, fun
- high-chroma yellow-orange: joy, stimulating
- high-chroma green: infancy, lively

Color Scheme: near tetrad plus neutral

The high-chroma primary, secondary, and tertiary colors found within this mark are well suited for the content. Most children of daycare age tend to gravitate toward these types of color schemes, and in this scenario it is learned behavior.

SYDNEY 2000 OLYMPICS

Designers: Michael Bryce and Ron Hurley
Creative Director: Michael Bryce
Studio: Minale Bryce Design Strategy

Associative Color Response:
• high-chroma blue: lively, mature
• high-chroma yellow: welcome
• black: elegant, powerful
• high-chroma green: motion, hope
• high-chroma red: energizing

Color Scheme: primary, secondary, plus neutral

Indexical references to a geographic location are an excellent way to create a symbol-based mark. Inspired by the Sydney Opera House and Aboriginal art, the Sydney 2000 Olympics mark captures the spirit of a nation.

OH! OXYGEN

Studio: AdamsMorioka

Associative Color Response:
• black: powerful, elegant
• neutral gray: quality
• high-chroma red-violet: exciting, flamboyant
• pastel red-violet: refined
• mid-range red-violet: charming
• pastel pink: sweet
• mid-range pink: restrain
• high-chroma red: brilliant
• dark blue: credible
• high-chroma blue: dignified, lively
• pastel blue: pleasure
• pastel red-orange: gentle
• mid-range red-orange: inviting
• high-chroma red-orange: brilliant, intense
• pastel yellow-green: tart
• mid-range yellow-green: strength
• high-chroma yellow-green: sharp, bold
• pastel yellow-orange: pleasant
• mid-range yellow-orange: warmth
• high-chroma yellow-orange: powerful, energy

Color Scheme: monochromatic with tinting plus neutral with tinting

A simplistic color palette is created in each of these color studies. Black and neutral gray act as the governor between each study presented. The high-chroma hue (blue, red-violet, red, red-orange, yellow-green, and yellow-orange) is tinted to create movement from left to right. Each color combination creates a different associative response.

THE 9TH ANNUAL SERIOUS MOONLIGHT RIO STYLE

Designer/Creative Director:
Francheska Guerrero
Studio: Conversant Studios

Associative Color Response:
- high-chroma yellow: agreeable, welcomed
- pastel pink: energetic, joyful
- mid-range pink: sentimental
- high-chroma pink: stimulating
- high-chroma red: energizing

Color Scheme: two points of a triad with tinting

Harking back to the psychedelic past, this retro-style logomark uses a high-chroma color scheme coupled with font selection to help create visual tension and kinetic energy.

PODRAVINA

Designer/Art Director: Toni Adamic
Studio: Elevator

Associative Color Response:
- mid-range blue: refreshing
- high-chroma blue: honesty, strength
- dark blue: credible
- high-chroma blue-violet: expensive, regal

Color Scheme: simple analogous with tinting and shading

The podravina logomark is a refreshing example of a simplistic color palette that is wonderfully executed. The way in which the colors are formally laid out within the mark creates a rotating progression of color that energizes the mark and gives it kinetic energy.

TRAVEL PORT

Studio: Hornall Anderson Design Works

Associative Color Response:
- high-chroma red: energizing, active
- high-chroma yellow-orange: excitement
- neutral gray: quality, passion
- high-chroma blue: honesty, pleasant
- high-chroma green: spring

Color Scheme: near tetrad plus neutral (tinted)

Opposition is an excellent way to create visual tension within a mark. The duality found between "Travel," in neutral gray, and "Port," in high-chroma primaries and tertiary hues, creates a counterbalance that allows one half to play off the other. Note how "Port" jumps off the page and "Travel" settles back, creating a visual foundation.

BABY BASICS

Studio: Essex Two

Associative Color Response:
- black: basic
- high-chroma blue: lively, happy
- high-chroma red: stimulating, fun
- high-chroma yellow-orange: joy, stimulating
- high-chroma green: infancy, lively

Color Scheme: near tetrad plus neutral

The Baby Basics logotype is well suited for this kind of color scheme. Muddy and dirty colors are not favored by children of this age.

BEAST OF THE EAST.NET

Designers: Kristin Sommese and Lanny Sommese
Studio: Sommese Design

Associative Color Response:
- black: powerful
- neutral gray: quality, passion
- high-chroma blue: lively, strength
- high-chroma red: brilliant, aggressive
- high-chroma yellow-green: strength

Color Scheme: random plus neutral with tinting

Beast of The East.Net is an excellent example of a logomark that does not follow a standardized color scheme. However, this mark does follow learned color association—red for tongue, white for teeth, black for dog, and blue for the environment.

BRENT PONG PHOTOGRAPHY

Designer: Suling Pong

Associative Color Response:
- dark orange: exhilarating
- high-chroma blue: lively
- dark yellow: active
- high-chroma red-violet: elegant
- high-chroma green: motion

Color Scheme: random with shading

The logotype is an excellent example of using shading to tone down the chroma level of the hues used. Not every mark created requires hues that use the highest level of chroma within their respective families.

CROSS CONDITIONING SYSTEMS

Designer: Justin Deister
Studio: Uppercase Design

Associative Color Response:
- high-chroma red-violet: exciting
- high-chroma yellow-orange: growing
- high-chroma blue-green: pristine, pure
- high-chroma red: energizing
- black: powerful, basic, elegant

Color Scheme: triad with red plus neutral

The directional flow of a mark is as important as any other formal and conceptual aspects. A mark that has a downward or backward flow will create a negative impact on the viewer.

SHARP PIXEL

Studio: Sharp Pixel

Associative Color Response:
- high-chroma red: energizing, active
- high-chroma pink: stimulating
- pastel pink: delicate, energetic
- black: powerful, basic, elegant

Color Scheme: monochromatic plus neutral

The sharp pixel logomark is a showcase of restraint. Using both a monochromatic color study and a modular system induces visual consistency that represents a corporate feel. The typeface chosen harmonizes with the anatomical structure of the mark, visually creating an overall masterpiece.

FRENCH LEAVE RESORT

Designers: Kristin Sommese and Lanny Sommese
Studio: Sommese Design

Associative Color Response:
- pastel blue: pleasure, peaceful, quiet
- pastel yellow-green: calm, natural
- pastel pink: comfortable, cozy
- pastel yellow-orange: pleasant
- black: powerful, basic, elegant

Color Scheme: near tetrad using primaries and tertiary with shading

This beautifully constructed mark, using substitution, was created for a resort on the island of Eleuthera in the Bahamas. Indexically referencing the beauty of the insect life found on the island, and the cultural center the resort represents to tourists and indigenous people alike, this mark symbolizes the atmosphere of the resort. A near tetrad using primary and tertiary pastel hues adds to the colorful nature of the mark.

ICC CRICKET WORLD CUP: WEST INDIES 2007

Designers: Dean Power and Michail Kowal
Creative Director: Michael Bryce
Studio: Minale Bryce Design Strategy

Associative Color Response:
- high-chroma blue: strength
- high-chroma yellow-orange: drive
- high-chroma red: intense
- black: powerful, basic, elegant

Color Scheme: primaries and tertiary hues plus neutral

This highly energetic mark is beautifully conceived through the high-chroma colors chosen and the agitation of line work.

Six+ Colors

Six+ color marks are relatively new. In the past
they were most often seen in the television and film
industries. Today, from "mom and pop" businesses to
large corporations, multicolored marks are influencing
how graphic designers create logos and how consumers
interact with businesses. No longer constrained by
astronomical commercial printing costs, a new color
vernacular is taking hold. This is reshaping the way
in which designers think about the creation of a mark;
a logo is now considered in terms of the context in
which it is used and the influence it has.

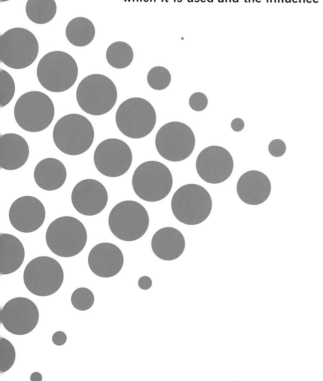

In addition, graphic design is no longer confined to
a geographical location and local vendors. A graphic
designer may have a closer working relationship with
a printer on the other side of the world than the printer
next door. The ability to communicate, interact, and
purchase 24/7 worldwide has led to dramatic price
reductions in printing and to more companies doing
a larger share of their business over the Internet,
and both changes have influenced the amount of
color found within a typical mark. A mark may still
be designed first in one or two colors, but if a designer
is worth his or her salt, the logo will also incorporate
multiple colors for every kind of scenario.

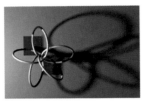

SECOND ANNUAL WORLD MILITARY GAMES

Designer: Boris Ljubicic

Associative Color Response:
• high-chroma green: motion
• high-chroma blue: lively, upward
• high-chroma red: intense, energizing
• high-chroma yellow: welcome
• black: powerful
• white: purity

Color Scheme: primary and secondary hues plus neutral and white

The Second Annual World Military Games are similar in spirit and content to the Olympics. As a point of departure and inspiration, five interlocking rings were chosen as the basic geometric shape. In contrast to the Olympics design, these rings were tightly grouped and rendered three-dimensionally into the shape of an open flower—an oxymoron of strong and delicate. Each color (red, blue, yellow, green, and black) on the ring signifies the continents, while the red squares signify the geographical location of the games—in this case, Croatia.

DLU: DON'T LET UP

Art Director: Chevonne Woodard
Studio: Chevonne Woodard Design

Associative Color Response:
• high-chroma red: brilliant
• dark red: strong
• black: powerful
• dark gray: classic
• neutral gray: quality

Color Scheme: one hue with shading plus neutral with tinting

The DLU mark is an excellent example of creating numerous hues using two inks.

MLJET

Designer: Boris Ljubicic

Associative Color Response:
• high-chroma green: life
• high-chroma red: brilliant
• high-chroma blue-green: pristine, pure
• high-chroma blue: lively
• dark blue-green: natural
• neutral gray: quality

Color Scheme: complex analogous color palette with red accent, tints, and shades plus neutral

This logotype captures the Mediterranean feel of Croatia's coastline. A combination of high-chroma, dark, and natural hues is used in an indexical manner to reference the landscape.

LIQUID FUXION

Designer: Michael Gray

Associative Color Response:
• light gray: quality
• dark gray: wise
• black: powerful

Color Scheme: achromatic

The line work found in this logomark coupled with the typography creates a contemporary design that symbolizes the digital age. The achromatic color palette helps to simplify and counterbalance this highly complex design.

WASSERMAN MEDIA GROUP

Studio: AdamsMorioka

Associative Color Response:
- high-chroma orange: curiosity, communication
- high-chroma yellow: energy
- high-chroma yellow-green: strength
- high-chroma green: motion
- high-chroma blue: lively
- high-chroma blue-green: forward
- high-chroma violet: power
- earth-tone red: earthy
- dark orange: exhilarating
- dark green: nature
- neutral gray: quality

Color Scheme: random—primary, secondary, and tertiary hues with tinting and shading plus neutral

This colorful logomark is gloriously vivid. The high-intensity hues coupled with dark and pastel colors create a complex hue hierarchy that is truly amazing. If all the hues used within the color palette were of a high-chroma color scheme, the palette would not work. This is an excellent example of creating a counterbalance between high-chroma, pastel, and dark hues.

JOHNSON COUNTY LIBRARY FOUNDATION

Designer: Eric Looney
Art Directors: Eric Looney and Margaret Bowker
Studio: GouldEvans

Associative Color Response:
- high-chroma orange: curiosity, communication
- high-chroma yellow-orange: stimulating
- mid-range orange, pastel orange: inviting
- neutral gray: quality
- white: bright

Color Scheme: simple analogous with tinting plus neutral (tinted)

The color palette used for this logomark is an excellent example of practical color use—stretching the palette. In reality, this logomark could be produced with two inks and a type reversal.

SAN-GI KYO STAR

Designer: Massaaki Omura

Associative Color Response:
- high-chroma blue-green: pristine
- pastel blue-green: pure

Color Scheme: monochromatic with tinting

Within this mark, one ink is used with tinting to create an array of colors.

WORLDCENTRIC MEDIA

Designer: Jessica Flores

Associative Color Response:
- high-chroma violet: power, dignified
- high-chroma blue-green: pristine
- high-chroma yellow-orange: excitement
- high-chroma yellow-green: sharp
- high-chroma red: brilliant
- dark orange: exhilarating
- high-chroma green: motion
- dark yellow: active
- high-chroma blue-violet: powerful
- black: strong

Color Scheme: hyper-complex near analogous color palette

Through the use of scale, this modular logomark creates an (unusual) active symmetrical composition. Most symmetrical compositions are created to make the viewer's eye rest. This mark, however, uses high-chroma hues coupled with scale and placement to create an energetic mark.

SMS FOODS

Designer: Boris Ljubicic

Associative Color Response:
- mid-range green: classic
- dark green: natural
- neutral gray: quality
- dark gray: expensive
- high-chroma red: energizing
- high-chroma orange: healing

Color Scheme: primary and secondary hues plus neutral (tinted)

The Slogan for SMS Foods is "A Message from Nature"—a gastronomic delight that uses only natural products (fish, olives, vegetables, and fruits) from the Adriatic coastal region of Dalmatia. The color use in the SMS logotype is both symbolic and iconic. The two gray and two green hues reference fish scales and olive leaves, whereas the red and orange symbolically represent edible foods. Both the high-chroma red and orange have an excellent appetite rating, with an associative taste of very sweet.

POWI

Designer: George White
Art Director: Mark Sackett
Studio: Sackett Design

Associative Color Response:
- mid-range blue-violet: classic
- dark blue: credible
- dark orange: exhilarating
- earth-tone orange: sound
- dark red: mature
- dark red-violet: exciting

Color Scheme: complementary warm and cool colors with overprinting

The Powi logotype is an outstanding use of overprinting to stretch the hues to make them look as though more ink is being used. Note where the inks overprint to create additional hues.

PACE INTERNATIONAL

Studio: Hornall Anderson Design Works

Associative Color Response:
- green: life, motion
- green-yellow: lemony, fruity
- yellow: vigorous, inspiring
- yellow-orange: drive, goal
- orange: healing, tasty
- red: energizing, powerful

Color Scheme: complementary (red and green) plus near analogous

The Pace International logomark is highly kinetic in a circular upward motion. This is brought to bear through the choice of high-chroma hues and scale.

CROATIAN NATIONAL TOURIST BOARD

Designer: Boris Ljubicic

Associative Color Response:
- high-chroma red: stimulating
- high-chroma red-orange: energizing
- high-chroma orange: healing
- high-chroma blue: relaxed
- high-chroma violet: memories
- high-chroma yellow-green: strength

Color Scheme: direct/near/split complementary

The color palette chosen for the logotype is quite intense. Designer Boris Ljubicic wanted to convey a Mediterranean paradise where people around the world could relax and enjoy themselves. The hand-lettered typography found within the logotype helps to create a cohesive whole, no matter what the mark is juxtaposed with.

SUN SHINE: DICK LEE'S PROJECT

Designer: Audrey Koh
Studio: Plastic Soldier Factory

Associative Color Response:
- mid-range yellow-orange: good spirits
- high-chroma orange: cheerfulness
- high-chroma pink: stimulating
- pastel pink: energetic
- mid-range red-violet: flamboyant
- mid-range violet: nostalgic
- high-chroma blue-green: young
- high-chroma yellow-green: bold

Color Scheme: random

This retro psychedelic-style logomark is superbly crafted through the use of color, shape, and typographic specimen. A visual consistency is achieved through using the hues specified at the same or nearly the same chroma value.

COLORS YOU FEEL

Studio: Sharp Pixel

Associative Color Response:
- dark yellow: stimulating
- high-chroma blue: relaxed
- dark yellow: active
- high-chroma orange: healing
- dark orange: exhilarating
- pastel blue: refreshing
- black: elegant
- neutral gray: quality
- dark gray: wise, solid

Color Scheme: direct complementary with yellow accent plus neutral and tinting

These modular-system logomarks are a fine example of using a complex complementary color palette within a sequence of 2, 2, 2 (two yellows, two oranges, and two blues)— not including black and its tints. The circular logomark is not complementary but random, and is also modular, using cropping, scaling, overprinting, hue replacement, and sequencing (2, 2, 2) to create a highly kinetic mark. This is evident in both the black and white mark as well as the color.

MILLENNIUM FOODS

Designer: Erik Potter
Creative Directors: Laura Titzer and Andrew Salyer
Studio: Fahrenheit Design

Associative Color Response:
- high-chroma yellow-green: bold
- high-chroma yellow-orange: enterprise
- high-chroma orange: cleanliness
- high-chroma dark orange: stirring
- earth-tone red: earthy
- neutral gray: quality

Color Scheme: complex analogous with green accent plus neutral and tinting

The Millennium Foods logomark is a superb example of choosing a color palette that has an excellent appetite rating. This complex analogous color palette is made up primarily of high-chroma (sweet to very sweet) orange hues. Choosing the appropriate color palette for marks that represent food should be the first course of action when developing the mark.

YOUN

Designer/Art Director: Kyeong-Wan Youn
Studio: Youn Graphics & Interactive Design

Associative Color Response:
- high-chroma orange: cheerfulness
- high-chroma yellow-green: bold
- high-chroma blue: lively
- high-chroma red: intense
- dark gray: professional
- neutral gray: quality
- black: powerful

Color Scheme: near tetrad plus neutral with tinting

The Youn logomark is an excellent example of using cool and warm colors. Within this mark, designer Kyeong-Wan Youn sets up a binary opposition using the two extremes: black (the coolest color) and high-chroma warm hues (red, orange, and yellow-green). This makes the logomark pop.

CIRCLE OF LOVE

Designer/Art Director: Handy Atmali
Studio: HA Design

Associative Color Response:
- pastel blue: pleasure
- high-chroma yellow-orange: powerful
- high-chroma orange: happy
- high-chroma yellow-green: new growth
- high-chroma red-violet: exciting
- black: quality

Color Scheme: tetrad with yellow-orange accent plus neutral

The physicality of the composition and color choice create a highly kinetic mark that encapsulates the subject matter. The light, airy typography harmonizes well with the scaled circular forms and high-chroma hues evoking the feelings of first love.

REBELMAIL

Designer: Ken Kelleher

Associative Color Response:
- dark gray: professional
- neutral gray: quality
- light gray: classic
- dark red: mature
- high-chroma orange: growing
- pastel orange: inviting

Color Scheme: one hue with tinting and shading plus neutral (tinted)

The mail delivery mark uses two inks to create a multitude of colors. Speed lines and drop shadows are used to help create a 3D allusion on a 2D plane.

NAIVA

Studio: Boris Ljubicic

Associative Color Response:
- high-chroma blue: lively
- high-chroma yellow-orange: stimulating
- high-chroma red: active, cheer
- high-chroma blue-violet: powerful
- pastel blue-violet: happy
- high-chroma blue-green: fresh

Color Scheme: random high-chroma hues with pastel accent

This modular-system logotype uses similarity of form, rotation, placement, and high-chroma hues to create continuity within the mark.

ANCHORBALL

Designer: Ken Kelleher

Associative Color Response:
- high-chroma blue-green: pristine
- high-chroma yellow-green: bold
- high-chroma yellow-orange: drive
- pastel blue-green: firm
- mid-range blue-violet: charming
- pastel blue-violet: elegant

Color Scheme: random with sequential pattern

Although this may appear to be a random color palette, there is a logic to the hues chosen. Yellow-orange is two steps away from yellow-green, which itself is two steps away from blue-green, and that is two steps from blue-violet. When dealing with this kind of color complexity, using other aspects in 2D design and applying them to practical color use is a prudent measure.

COMMUNITY UNITY

Designer: Erik Chrestensen
Studio: Chrestensen Design Works

Associative Color Response:
- dark blue-violet: classic
- pastel blue-violet: cool
- earth-tone red: sound
- dark orange: stirring
- neutral gray: quality

Color Scheme: near complementary with tinting and shading

This logomark is a superb example of stretching color, through the use of gradients, and tinting, to make it seem as though there are numerous hues.

DEERFOOT MEADOWS

Designer: Erik Chrestensen
Studio: Chrestensen Design Works

Associative Color Response:
- high-chroma red: dignified
- dark red: refined
- earth-tone red: rustic
- high-chroma yellow-orange: luxurious
- pastel yellow-orange: pleasant
- black: powerful

Color Scheme: two points of a tetrad with tinting and shading plus neutral

The Deerfoot logotype is a wonderful example of using the appropriate colors and typefaces with the content to achieve the desired visual correspondence.

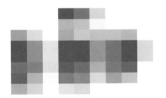

MEDICAL CHANNEL

Designer: Massaaki Omura

Associative Color Response:
- high-chroma pink: stimulating
- pastel pink: energetic
- high-chroma orange: growing
- dark orange: exhilarating, inspiring
- high-chroma red-orange: hope
- dark red-orange: serious

Color Scheme: simple analogous with tinting

In this digitally rendered mark, the abstract form is made up from a modular system (squares) to create a contemporary mark that references high-definition broadcasting.

UMEHACHI

Designer: Minato Ishikawa

Associative Color Response:
- high-chroma red-violet: exciting
- pastel red-violet: select
- high-chroma orange: healing
- dark orange: stimulating
- pastel orange: enticing
- earth-tone red: warm-hearted
- black: powerful

Color Scheme: near complex analogous with tinting and shading plus neutral

This modular-system logomark is more organic than most. The round circular shapes are varied in form from one another and placed asymmetrically. This creates a more natural mark.

COLOR PALETTE: SUNDIAL OF COLORS

Studio: AdamsMorioka

Associative Color Response:
- high-chroma yellow: noble
- dark yellow: active
- dark yellow-green: new growth
- pastel yellow-green: sharp
- pastel green: calm
- high-chroma blue-green: cool
- dark blue-green: young
- high-chroma blue: lively
- dark blue: credible
- pastel blue-green: pure
- pastel red-violet: charming
- pastel pink: tender
- high-chroma pink: excitement
- high-chroma red: brilliant
- dark orange: exhilarating
- high-chroma orange: tasty
- high-chroma yellow-orange: joy
- pastel orange: gentle
- pastel earth-tone red: warm
- earth-tone red: wholesome
- earth-tone black: powerful

Color Scheme: hyper complex random with tinting and shading

This modular-system logomark has 24 units. Each unit is in the shape of a wedge and has its own specified hue. The typography is purposely simplified to counterbalance the complexity of the mark.

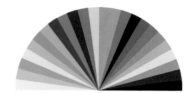

GLENSHORE

Designer: Nate Burgos

Associative Color Response:
- high-chroma yellow-green: bold
- high-chroma green: life
- dark orange: stirring
- high-chroma orange: growing
- high-chroma blue: pleasing
- black: elegant

Color Scheme: random with high-chroma hues plus neutral

In this logo, harmony is achieved through primarily a high-chroma-hue color palette. Black and dark orange are implemented to achieve an accent counterbalance.

GLENSHORE

SO-NET

Designer: Massaaki Omura

Associative Color Response:
- high-chroma yellow: energy
- dark yellow: active
- dark yellow-orange: stimulating
- dark orange: moving
- high-chroma green: life
- dark green: growth
- black: powerful

Color Scheme: near complex analogous with shading plus neutral

Note the opposition occurring within the logomark. The typography acts as a flat 2D surface to counterbalance the 3D mark. The hues found within the 3D mark are warm, whereas the black hue is cool.

FOZZY

Designer: Stefan G. Bucher
Studio: 344

Associative Color Response:
- gold: expensive, warm
- silver: valuable
- black: powerful

Color Scheme: random plus neutral

This unusual logotype is designed to have the look and feel of a hood ornament. This is accomplished primarily through the choice of hues.

SAGENT

Designer: Carlo Irigoyen
Art Director: Brenda Spivack
Studio: Red Table

Associative Color Response:
- high-chroma yellow: agreeable
- high-chroma yellow-orange: stimulating
- high-chroma orange: healing
- high-chroma red-orange: active
- high-chroma red: intense
- high-chroma yellow-green: new growth
- high-chroma green: life
- black: elegant

Color Scheme: complex analogous plus neutral

In this beautifully constructed color palette, the Sagent mark uses size and placement to harmonize the mark with the typography.

SAGENT

Designer: Brenda Spivack
Studio: Red Table

Associative Color Response:
- dark green: growth
- dark yellow: active
- pastel yellow: sunshine
- mid-range yellow-orange: energy
- dark yellow-orange: inspiring

Color Scheme: near analogous with shading

The flat-pattern illustration found within this logomark is an excellent example of substitution—the flower is substituted in place of the bowl in the lowercase "g."

Lighting Council
AUSTRALIA

LIGHTING COUNCIL: AUSTRALIA

Designer: Raymond Koo
Creative Director: Michael Bryce
Studio: Minale Bryce Design Strategy

Associative Color Response:
- mid-range red-violet: refined
- high-chroma red: brilliant
- high-chroma orange: loud
- high-chroma yellow-orange: excitement
- high-chroma yellow-green: sunlight
- pastel blue: pleasure
- high-chroma blue: lively
- black: powerful

Color Scheme: double direct/ near complementary

The spectrum of colors and physicality of form created for this mark is well suited to the content. Scale and hue are used within this system to create radiating outward movement.

WHO ARE WE

Designer: Manar Al-Muftah
Art Director: Peter Martin

Associative Color Response:
- pastel yellow-orange: pleasant
- mid-range orange: gentle
- dark red: refined, taste
- pastel blue: quiet
- pastel blue-green: calm
- mid-range blue-green: pure
- high-chroma blue-green: new, pristine
- black: elegant

Color Scheme: direct/near complementary with shading plus neutral (tinted)

This Arabic logotype is meant to look like a shisha or hubbly-bubbly water pipe, and is used here as a cultural identifier. It has been superbly executed. In the top version, the tan hue is meant to reference the landscape found in this region (the Arabian Peninsula).

HARVEST-DRIVE

Designer: Massaaki Omura

Associative Color Response:
- high-chroma yellow-orange: excitement, stimulating, fun
- high-chroma orange: happy, healing, growing
- high-chroma red-orange: energizing
- high-chroma pink/red: exciting

Color Scheme: complex analogous

Although this may not seem to be a six-color mark (using only two inks) the gradient/split fountain found within the logo design creates a multitude of hues. This is an excellent example of stretching colors to help create movement within a mark.

APERIOS

Designer: Massaaki Omura

Associative Color Response:
- pastel blue: refreshing
- high-chroma blue: lively, electric
- high-chroma blue-violet: elegant
- black: powerful

Color Scheme: complex analogous plus neutral

This complex analogous color palette uses tinting and shading (through the use of gradients) to create a 3D illusion on a 2D plane. The 3D illusion is minimized by the choice of cool hues.

CREATIVE ENVIRONMENTS OF HOLLYWOOD

Designer: Brenda Spivack
Studio: Red Table

Associative Color Response:
- high-chroma blue: dignity
- mid-range blue: life
- dark blue: service
- dark gray: professional
- neutral gray: classic
- black: strong

Color Scheme: one hue with tinting and shading plus neutral (tinted)

A 3D illusion is established through two-point perspective, lighting, and hue control to create a very dynamic mark. The 3D illusion is intensified by juxtaposing it with a flat object (the company name).

ARCHILAB 2004

Studio: Thonik Design

Associative Color Response:
- high-chroma orange: warm
- mid-range pink: soft
- mid-range red-violet: elegant
- dark red: taste
- black: powerful
- dark gray: professional
- neutral gray: quality

Color Scheme: near analogous with tinting and shading plus neutral (tinted)

This mark was designed for a group of architects exhibiting their work in 2004. The design of the modular-system mark was carried out by the use of proportionate panels throughout the exhibit. Thonik Design wanted to create a strong identity that united all the members who were participating. In the final exhibit, 80 panels were used, each with its own hue.

KID BITS

Studio: Essex Two

Associative Color Response:
- high-chroma red: brilliant
- mid-range orange: general
- dark orange: exhilarating
- high-chroma yellow-green: new growth
- mid-range blue-violet: charming
- pastel blue: clean
- pastel blue-violet: delicate
- high-chroma blue: happy

Color Scheme: direct complementary with yellow-green and red accent, tinting and shading

The physicality of form and color hues chosen creates a highly kinetic mark that metaphorically represents the atmosphere associated with a daycare center. This is a wonderful mark that illustrates how color can add content.

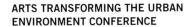

ARTS TRANSFORMING THE URBAN ENVIRONMENT CONFERENCE

Designers: Ned Drew, Brenda McManus, and Dale Garcia
Creative Director: Ned Drew

Associative Color Response:
- high-chroma orange: healing
- mid-range orange: enticing, inviting
- dark orange: stimulating
- mid-range pink: soft
- dark red: develop
- neutral gray: quality
- dark gray: cultured
- black: powerful

Color Scheme: complex analogous plus neutral (tinted)

In the Arts Transforming The Urban Environment logo, color is injected into the mark through a slow transition from left to right. This treatment symbolizes how the arts can help revitalize a depressed area.

DISNEY'S FANTASIA SHOP

Designer/Art Director: David Ferrell
Creative Director: David Riley
Studio: DR+A

Associative Color Response:
- high-chroma yellow-orange: stimulating
- high-chroma orange: happy
- high-chroma red: fun
- high-chroma red-violet: exciting
- high-chroma blue-violet: classic
- dark orange: exhilarating
- black: powerful

Color Scheme: hypercomplex, near analogous color palette

The Disney's Fantasia Shop mark is a superb example of matching hues with subject matter. Masterfully created, the high-chroma hues fuse in a kinetic liveliness unsurpassed by many other marks.

E.M. PICNIC

Studio: Essex Two

Associative Color Response:
- high-chroma red: brilliant
- dark red: elegant
- high-chroma pink: exciting
- high-chroma yellow-green: fruity
- high-chroma green: growth
- dark green: nature
- black: powerful

Color Scheme: direct complementary plus neutral

Anytime a continuous-tone image is used to create a logomark for print-based design, a coarse screen pattern should be used. In this case, the mark is design for Web and motion graphics. If this mark were to be used in print, it would need to be printed using four-color process.

INDIANAPOLIS ZOO

Studio: Essex Two

Associative Color Response:
- high-chroma yellow-green: new growth
- high-chroma green: outdoorsy
- pastel blue: happy
- high-chroma blue: honesty
- high-chroma blue-violet: tender
- dark red-violet: life
- high-chroma blue-green: pristine
- earth-tone red: earthy
- dark gray: enduring
- neutral gray: quality
- black: elegant

Color Scheme: hypercomplex, near analogous color palette

When using photographs within logomarks, a coarse screen pattern or high-contrast image is advised. However, if the client is using the mark for Web, or is only going to print, for example, the stationery on a personal color printer, then it is perfectly fine. In an attempt to save money, many institutions are turning to self-publishing and printing via inkjet printers and the like.

PIECES

Designer: Inyoung Choi

Associative Color Response:
- earth-tone red: rustic
- earth tone: rooted
- dark orange: exhilarating
- high-chroma orange: autumn
- mid-range orange: inviting
- high-chroma yellow-orange: energy
- black: powerful

Color Scheme: near analogous with tinting and shading plus black

This unusual logotype is created through continuous-tone images. Harmony is achieved by creating a consistent color palette by using shading throughout the logotype.

LIVING WELL WITH CANCER

Studio: Bremmer & Goris Communications

Associative Color Response:
- high-chroma green: life
- high-chroma yellow-orange: healthy
- high-chroma red: energizing
- high-chroma blue: dignity
- pastel green: empathy
- black: powerful

Color scheme: direct/near complementary/ tertiary with tinting plus neutral

A superb color palette—the symbiotic relationship between the color palette, script typeface, and overall shape create a lively and energetic mark that is most appropriate to the subject matter.

SONY LIFE

Designer: Massaaki Omura

Associative Color Response:

- high-chroma blue-green: pristine
- mid-range blue-green: pure
- pastel blue-green: lively
- high-chroma blue-violet: powerful
- mid-range blue-violet: refined
- pastel blue-violet: select
- dark gray: professional

Color Scheme: two points of the split complementary or near analogous plus neutral

In the Sony Life logomark, gradients are used most effectively to create kinetic energy or movement within the mark.

SONY ECO PLAZA

Designer: Massaaki Omura

Associative Color Response:

- high-chroma blue-green: pristine
- pastel blue: lively
- high-chroma blue-violet: powerful
- neutral gray: quality

Color Scheme: analogous with tinting plus neutral (tinted)

The layered information found within this logomark is laid out to create an asymmetrical composition within the circle. This creates an intense amount of movement within the mark. The reversed letterform (white, in this case) is used as a navigational device to pull the eye in and through the mark.

ANEMONE

ANEMONE

Designer: Mark Raebel
Studio: Arsenal Design

Associative Color Response:

- pastel red-violet: refined
- pastel gray: classic
- pastel blue-violet: fantasy
- pastel dark pink: soft
- pastel pink: cute
- black: elegant

Color Scheme: near analogous

Harmony of form is achieved through a similarity of line work and pastel color use. By using soft pastel hues, the mark does not become heavy-handed and achieves a sophisticated appearance appropriate for the makeup it produces.

AEROBLOKS, TINKER MINDS, INC.

Designer: Mark Raebel
Studio: Arsenal Design

Associative Color Response:

- high-chroma pink: aggressive
- high-chroma red: brilliant
- high-chroma yellow-orange: fun
- high-chroma yellow-green: strength
- high-chroma green: lively
- earth-tone red: warm
- high-chroma red-violet: exciting
- neutral gray: quality

Color Scheme: complementary with accent plus neutral

Both of these marks are superb examples of overprinting. When using overprinting, set up color matrixes in Photoshop and apply Multiply in the layers dialog box. This allows for visual verification of the overprinting hues—by doing so, no surprises will occur on press.

EXPODESIGN: KOREA-JAPAN FRIENDSHIP YEAR 2005

Designer: Inyoung Choi

Associative Color Response:
- high-chroma blue-violet: fantasy
- high-chroma blue: pleasing
- mid-range blue: glory
- high-chroma red: charming
- high-chroma red-orange: excitement
- high-chroma orange: childlike
- high-chroma yellow-orange: joy
- black: basic

Color Scheme: complementary with tinting plus neutral

This superbly executed mark is cleverly conjoined to create a joyful atmosphere. Gradient hues are used to create an innocent, glowing, and loving mood.

EXPODESIGN: VISIT GYEONGGI-KOREA 2005

Designer: Inyoung Choi

Associative Color Response:
- high-chroma blue-violet: fantasy
- high-chroma blue: pleasing
- high-chroma red: charming
- high-chroma yellow-orange: joy
- neutral gray: quality
- black: powerful

Color Scheme: random plus neutral with tinting

The high-chroma hues counterbalanced with white, black, and gray create a unique color combination that is highly kinetic.

BOOKS@VBA.ORG

Designer: Caroline Cardwell

Associative Color Response:
- high-chroma dark red: develop
- high-chroma blue-violet: pleasure
- high-chroma green: lively
- high-chroma yellow-orange: fun
- high-chroma blue: powerful
- high-chroma red: brilliant
- high-chroma red-violet: creative
- high-chroma yellow-green: new growth
- earth-tone orange: welcome
- high-chroma orange: growing
- dark blue-violet: credible
- high-chroma pink: stimulating
- mid-range green: classic
- high-chroma blue-green: new

Color Scheme: hyper-complex analogous with orange and orange-yellow complementary

If color sells a product then there is no finer example then this mark. A smorgasbord of high-chroma hues is used to portray a somewhat dry subject, creating a lively atmosphere. When using an array of colors within a design, it is best to start with traditional color palettes and then expand their hue base.

NUCLEAR LEMONADE

Designer: Caroline Cardwell

Associative Color Response:
- high-chroma yellow: agreeable
- high-chroma yellow-orange: exciting
- dark orange: exhilarating
- pastel blue: happy
- pastel blue-green: young
- black: powerful

Color Scheme: near complementary/tertiary

The primary colors for this logomark are yellow, yellow-orange, and dark orange. Each of these hues has an excellent appetite rating, with a taste association of sweet. The mark was designed for a bar in the San Francisco Bay area. The bar (Nuclear Lemonade) prides itself on using the latest liquor sensations and mixology, embracing creativity from their bartenders to create a hip and playful atmosphere.

Packaging: 3D Designs

Effective, practical color use is intrinsic to the process
of solving a graphic design problem. Without color,
products would lack differentiation and standout.
Color sells a product—it creates emotional responses
that can communicate well beyond the size, shape,
and scope of the product. Color has the ability
to transform and translate meaningful messages.

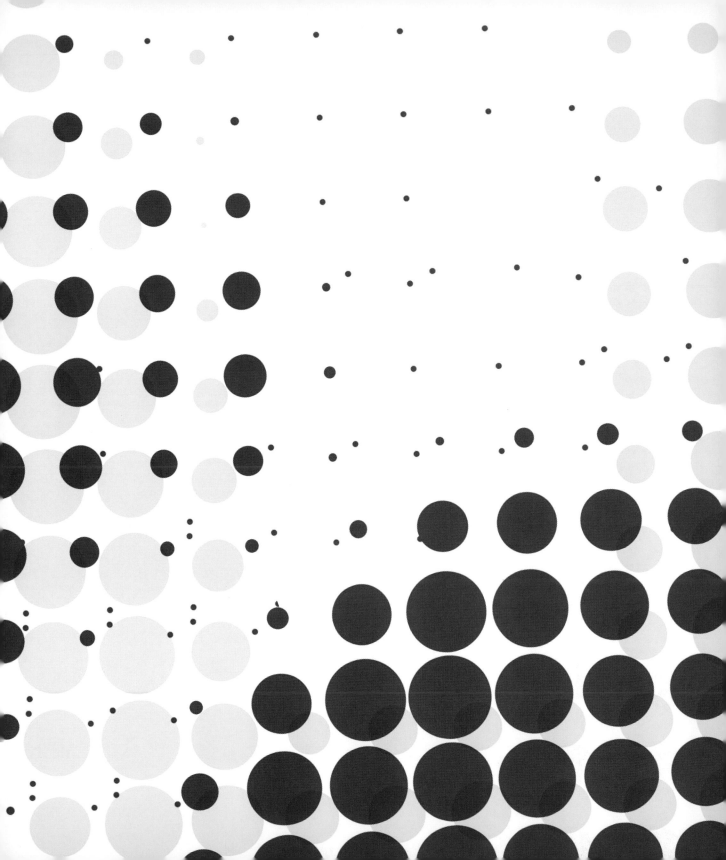

One & Two Colors

One- and two-color package design commonly has budgetary constraints limiting the number of hues that can be used. However, as demonstrated in this chapter, one- and two-color packaging requires a greater use of creativity—a mastering of 3D form, color, typography, image making, composition, and conceptual development. This is not to say that three- and four-color jobs do not possess the same qualities, however, a full-color iconic photograph is often used leaving no room for gestalt—the active participation of the audience.

Most often, when dealing with one- and two-color packaging, symbolic and indexical information is used, which leaves more to the imagination, and some stunning examples are found in this chapter. An underutilized marketing strategy for high-end design, one- and two-color package design can create striking visual separation on the shelf. It should be considered seriously every time a new design or campaign is being developed.

CURIOUS SOFA

Studio: REFLECTUR.COM

Associative Color Response:
• white: cleanliness, purity,
  clean, sterling

Color Scheme: one hue

The typographic specimens chosen
(Copperplate and script) reinforce the
timeless and classical nature of the design.

CURIOUS SOFA

Studio: REFLECTUR.COM

Associative Color Response:
• golden-yellow/beige family: harvest, classic,
  earthy, natural, soft
• blue-green family: pristine, pure, inner
  coolness, consistent
• earth-tone family: rustic, delicious,
  sheltering, warm

Color Scheme: two points of a triad
with shading

In this simple, elegant design harmony is
created through the use of overprinting on
a colored substrate, creating a bridge between
the light brown and the turquoise green.
Together the color palette, typography and
image create a timeless package design—
one that is appropriate for the content.

CURIOUS SOFA

Studio: REFLECTUR.COM

Associative Color Response:
• golden-yellow/beige family: harvest, classic,
  earthy, natural, soft
• earth-tone family: rustic, delicious,
  sheltering, warm

Color Scheme: one hue with tinting

The hand-held fan is not only beautifully
executed, but is also a brilliant concept,
harking back to a time where there was no
air conditioning—consistently reinforcing the
idea of a timeless and elegant experience.

CURIOUS SOFA

Studio: REFLECTUR.COM

Associative Color Response:
- golden-yellow/beige family: harvest, classic, earthy, natural, soft
- blue-green family: pristine, pure, inner coolness, consistent
- earth-tone family: rustic, delicious, sheltering, warm

Color Scheme: two points of a triad with shading

This simply constructed package design uses multiple layers to create a semiprecious object. Note that the sticker is attached to the cloth ribbon thus securing the contents during transportation. The additional layer of very thin and semitranslucent paper adds to the opening ritual before revealing the object inside.

CURIOUS SOFA

Studio: REFLECTUR.COM

Associative Color Response:
- golden-yellow/beige family: harvest, classic, earthy, natural, soft
- blue-green family: pristine, pure, inner coolness, consistent
- earth-tone family: rustic, delicious, sheltering, warm

Color Scheme: two points of a triad with shading

Sparing no expense, the labeling system for Curious Sofa is masterfully done. To help convey a timeless quality, the photograph of the woman's hair and face is not only styled after a popular 1920s haircut, but also manipulated to appear as though the image is etched.

ELIAS & GRACE

Studio: Aloof Design
Art Director: Sam Aloof
Designers: Andrew Scrase, Jon Hodkinson

Associative Color Response:
- earth-tone family: pleasant, warm
- blue-green family: pristine, pure, serious, lively

Color Scheme: two-points of a triad

Elias & Grace provides a modern, versatile approach to maternity and children's wear. Aloof Design created the brand identity, a range of playful packaging and garment labeling, business stationery, and a website. Luggage labels were created to price each garment and product, and to adorn the store's carrier bags and gift boxes. A die cut was utilized to emulate the relationship between parent and child, with colored glass beads and metal bells strung with brown linen thread to adorn the concept further. Note: Inks were mixed containing a high percentage of opaque white to lift the colors on the natural kraft material, and at the same time retaining a match to the brand-identity-specified hue.

VIRGIL'S FINE SOAPS

Studio: Fuelhaus
Art Director: Kellie Schroeder
Designer: Donovan Mafnas

Associative Color Response:
- high-chroma red family: active, cheer, joy, fun
- black: powerful, basic, neutral, classic

Color Scheme: one hue

Virgil's Fine Soaps is a classic example of a low-budget job superbly done. The design of the band gives the soap an "old-timey" feel without making the product look too verbose or overcrowded. The color palette is shifted from product to product by using different-colored paper—with the exception of red, this is often a seasonal color that printers have pre-mixed in stock, thus incurring no additional cost.

CAPSOLES

Studio: Exhibit A: Design Group
Art Director: Cory Ripley
Designers: Cory Ripley,
Robert Spofforth

Associative Color Response:

• high-chroma red family: brilliant, intense, active, cheer, joy, fun

Color Scheme: one hue plus shading (this includes the gray in the socks)

Color plays an important role for the Capsoles™ brand. The corporate colors (red and PANTONE® cool gray) were selected as the best combination to visually emote the term "sportmedical." In addition, these colors are easy to replicate in different methods of print production. The sleeve packaging ensures consumer confidence by soliciting/ reassuring a qualitative response of production confidence.

INTERSTATE PAPER

Art Director: Andrew Wong
Designers: Andrew Wong, Spy Lan
Copywriter: Andrew Wong

Associative Color Response:

• high-chroma red: brilliant, intense, energizing, sexy, dramatic, stimulating, joy, fun
• high-chroma green: motion, growth, fresh, lively, spring
• black: powerful, elegant, mysterious, heavy, basic
• silver: futuristic, cool, expensive, money, valuable, classic

Color Scheme: direct complementary with neutral

This unique package exploits the use of a three-dimensional color effects. When attempting to create work in this manner, the two plates—in this case green and red—need to be out of register in order for the three-dimensional effect to work. The more the image is out of register the deeper the 3D illusion. However, at a certain point this register effect will break down and flatten back out. It is best to work wearing 3D glasses when designing using this effect. Note: The opposition in color between the front and back of this beautifully executed design is masterfully done. The metallic silver printed on black opens to an orchestra of high-chroma colors on the reverse side—an excellent strategy for creating intrigue and kinetic energy throughout the piece.

U'LUVKA VODKA

Studio: Aloof Design
Art Director: Sam Aloof
Designers: Andrew Scrase,
Jon Hodkinson

Associative Color Response:
• silver family: cool, expensive, money, valuable, classic

Appetite Rating:
• silver family: excellent

Associative Taste:
• no associative tastes

Color Scheme: incongruous

This package design was litho printed using a solid custom ink mixed to match other packaging within this line. A silk-screen spot-varnish UV pattern was employed, adding elegance to the design, and a silver foil was used both for the logotype and mark. The combination of these techniques coupled with a black ribbon handle creates a highly sophisticated bag that is masterfully executed.

ALISON PRICE

Studio: Aloof Design
Art Director: Sam Aloof
Designers: Andrew Scrase,
Jon Hodkinson

Associative Color Response:
• high-chroma pink family: stimulates, aggressive, excitement, attention-getting

Appetite Rating:
• high-chroma pink family: excellent

Associative Taste:
• high-chroma pink: very sweet

Color Scheme: one hue

By using high-quality materials and printing, Aloof Design was able to create a memorable food package for private catering business Alison Price & Company to use as a teaser to entice prospective clients. The multifaceted canapé box is an Aloof in-house design. A solid magenta with a type reversal was employed. The logotype was then debossed to create a subtle shadow-and-texture effect. With a tabbed lid and envelope base, the box can be supplied flat and assembled by hand without any use of glue.

THE 12 BAR

Art Director: John T. Drew
Designer: Steve Gonsowski

Associative Color Response:
• earth-tone family: delicious, deep, rich, warm
• golden-yellow beige family: rich, sun, buttery, classic, natural

Appetite Rating:
• earth-tone family: excellent
• mid-range orange family: good to excellent
• golden-yellow/beige family: excellent

Associative Taste:
• mid-range orange family: sweet

Color Scheme: analogous with shading

This candy package is based conceptually on the 12-bar blues. The formal shape of the packaging is meant to resemble a harmonica, an instrument associated with the genre.

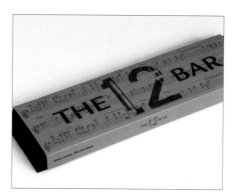

ASHFORD EYE DROPS

Studio: Midnite Oil
Art Director/Designer:
Mongkolsri Janjarasskul

Associative Color Response:
- pastel pink: intimate, active
- mid-range orange: gentle, entice, good spirits
- pastel green: innate, complete, calm, quiet, smoothing
- blue-green: pristine, pure, serious, cleanliness, incorruptible
- dark gray: cultured, professional, classic, expensive
- white: cleanliness, purity, clean

Color Scheme: one hue plus neutral

White is the dominant hue within this packaging series—an excellent choice for pharmaceutical products. In this case, white is created from the substrate's color, so technically this would be a two-color job. The other hues used within this system are for product identification.

DAHESH MUSEUM OF ART

Studio: Poulin + Morris

Associative Color Response:
- dark-red family: rich, elegant, refined, taste
- high-chroma yellow-orange: enterprise, drive, target, goal, luxuriance
- white: cleanliness, purity, clean, sterling, zeal, bright, awareness

Color Scheme: two points of a triad

This elegant and regal package design is a perfect color combination for the Dahesh Museum of Art. The oxblood red chosen was visually referenced from the museum's logotype—an academic artist's palette—and this is complemented by the yellow-orange, as the two colors harmonize through yellow and red. Note: visually referencing existing elements within a given environment is an excellent strategy for choosing colors within a color scheme or as a point of departure to invent a new palette.

WILD BITES

Studio: Exhibit A: Design Group
Art Director: Cory Ripley
Designers: Cory Ripley, Robert Spofforth

Associative Color Response:
- high-chroma red: brilliant, intense, energizing
- white: cleanliness, purity, clean
- earth tone: rustics, delicious, deep, rich, warm, folksy, rooted, life

Appetite Rating:
- high-chroma red: excellent
- white: excellent
- earth tone: good

Associative Taste:
- high-chroma red: very sweet

Color Scheme: monochromatic with tinting and shading

This packaging utilizes a vibrant, yet subtle color palette that conveys the character of the product—natural, fresh, organic, healthy, and gourmet. The four containers were printed simultaneously on a six-color press allowing each flavor its own specific PANTONE color. Each package uses a spot gloss varnish and dull aqueous coating for added visual depth.

CIAO BELLA

Studio: Wallace Church, Inc.
Creative Director: Stan Church

Associative Color Response:
- high-chroma pink: stimulates, aggressive, genial, exciting, happy, high, fun, excitement
- high-chroma orange: healing, tasty, cleanliness, cheerfulness
- high-chroma reddish purple: sweet taste, subtle, restlessness, prolongs life

Appetite Rating:
- high-chroma pink: excellent
- high-chroma orange: excellent

Associative Taste:
- high-chroma pink: very sweet
- high-chroma orange: very sweet

Color Scheme: near analogous

This high-chroma package series is intensely executed through hue. A symmetrical design is used to create a strong focal point (a snowflake) keeping the consumer's eye lodged in the center of the package. High-chroma hues are utilized to counterbalance the symmetrical design, giving the packages a kinetic energy through the use of hue.

BECKER SURF + SPORT

Studio: Jefferson Acker
Art Director: Glenn Sakamoto

Associative Color Response:
- dark-red family: rich, elegant, refined, taste, expensive, mature
- black: spatial, powerful, elegant, mysterious, heavy, basic, neutral
- white: refreshing, antiseptic, perfect balance, zeal, bright
- earth tone: delicious, deep, rich

Color Scheme: one hue with tinting plus neutral and white

This is a superb package design, printed with three hues—black, white, and brick red. The continuous-tone imagery was silkscreened using a crude halftone. The white and black hues are actually printed inks and have a distressed texture. White printed ink is uncommon—white is usually provided by the substrate—and thus can create a unique look and feel.

SCARBOROUGH AND COMPANY

Studio: Bohoy Design
Art Director: Johanna Bohoy, Susannah Jonas
Designer: Johanna Bohoy

Associative Color Response:
- pastel pink: soft, sweet, tender, joyful, beautiful, expressive, emotional
- pastel blue: pleasure, peace, calm, quiet
- mid-range red-purple: charming, elegant, select, refined, subtle
- high-chroma pink: stimulates, aggressive, genial, exciting, happy, high, fun, excitement
- dark green: nature, mountains, lakes, natural, mature growth
- dark orange: exhilarating, moving, inspiring, stirring, stimulating

Color Scheme: complementary with tinting, near complementary with tinting, and two points of a triad

This beautifully executed packaging references Art Nouveau styles. Many hues and color combinations are used to create this series, however, continuity is brought about through the consistent use of color tinting.

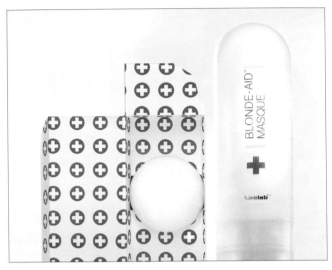

LUXELAB BLONDE-AID MASQUE

Studio: Dustin Edward Arnold
Art Director/Designer:
Dustin E. Arnold

Associative Color Response:
- high-chroma red: brilliant, intense, energizing, hope
- black: powerful, elegant, classic, strong
- white: purity, clean, life, refreshing, perfect balance

Color Scheme: one hue plus neutral and white

Blonde-Aid is a revitalizing conditioner formulated specifically for the special needs of blond hair. Keeping in line both with the salon's aesthetic and its strict modernist tastes, Blonde-Aid Masque is a salon-grade luxury product based on the needs of both stylists and their clients.

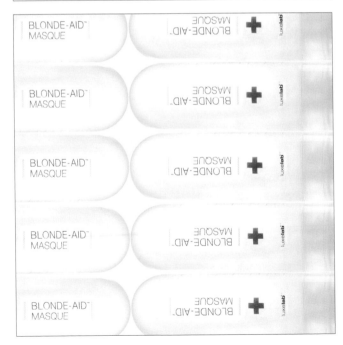

SHOOT BETTER

Studio: milkxhake
Art Director/Designer: milkxhake

Associative Color Response:
- high-chroma red: surging, brilliant, intense, energizing, sexy, dramatic, stimulating
- high-chroma orange: communication, cheerful, lively, exciting, bright, luminous
- white: zeal, bright, refreshing

Color Scheme: analogous with white

The redesign of a 35mm roll of film for *Cream*, an alternative-pop-culture magazine from Hong Kong—the slogan "Shoot better!" is a simple reminder before you load the film and press the shutter. By using warm, high-chroma colors that are not usually associated with this product, it visually separates itself from other packaging.

CREW

Art Director/Designer: Marcos Chavez

Associative Color Response:
- earth tone: delicious, deep, rich, warm
- blue-green: pristine, pure, serious, cleanliness, incorruptible

Color Scheme: near complementary with shading and white

The Crew shampoo bottle incorporates a masculine color scheme while at the same time choosing individual hues that are excellent for packaging. Note how the simplistic design is skillfully executed using symmetrical typographic techniques to create a strong focal point.

ZENZ THERAPY

Studio: Greydient
Designer: Morten Nielsen

Associative Color Response:
- silver: cool, expensive, money, valuable, classic
- dark gray: wise, cultured, mature, professional, classic, expensive, sophisticated, solid, enduring

Color Scheme: achromatic

The Zenz Therapy Conditioner bottle is a simple design—but classic. Beautifully executed, the vibrating oval symbolizes a human head, and at the same time is an energetic mark. The choice of silver and dark gray is masterfully executed, implying a sense of sophistication and quality.

WOW

Studio: Mary Hutchison Design LLC
Art Director/Designer:
Mary Chin Hutchison

Associative Color Response:
- high-chroma red: active, cheer, joy, fun
- high-chroma orange: cheerfulness, energizing, gregarious, friendly

Appetite Rating:
- high-chroma red: excellent
- high-chroma orange: excellent

Associative Taste:
- high-chroma red: very sweet
- high-chroma orange: very sweet

Color Scheme: analogous with white

The Wow cookie-dough buckets are quite unusual—this type of container is seldom used for this kind of product, and therefore stands out on the shelf. The choice of a white opaque container is an excellent one—using a clear container for cookie dough would not be recommended, as the natural color of the dough may have unwanted connotations.

AQUATANICA SPA

Studio: Doyle Partners

Associative Color Response:
- high-chroma bluish purple: expensive, regal, classic, powerful, tender, elegant
- black: powerful, elegant, mysterious
- white: refreshing, perfect balance, zeal, bright

Color Scheme: one hue plus tinting plus neutral

This specialty line of skincare products contains natural ingredients from the sea. A single strong color was chosen so the products would stand out visually from their competitors in a retail environment, where hundreds of bottles, jars, and tubes of skincare products compete for the buyer's attention. The imagery was inspired by Victorian cyanotypes.

CAPSOLES

Studio: Exhibit A: Design Group
Art Director: Cory Ripley
Designers: Cory Ripley,
Robert Spofforth

Associative Color Response:
- dark green: nature, mountains, lakes, natural, mature growth
- white: cleanliness, purity, clean, sterling

Color Scheme: near analogous

An excellent example of simplicity, the Capsoles Foot Emulsion uses color association and/or learned behavioral effects to imbue the bottle with the appropriate colors. Note how the plastic bottle has a large end-cap so that it can be stored cap down—a perfect solution for any liquid.

ARTIVA DESIGN

Studio: Artiva Design
Art Directors/Designers:
Davide Sossi, Daniele De Batte
Illustrator: Daniele De Batte

Associative Color Response:
- white: cleanliness, purity, clean, sterling
- high-chroma red: brilliant, intense, energizing
- silver: cool, expensive

Color Scheme: one hue plus neutral, white, and silver

This unique self-promotional package is cleverly conceived and wonderfully executed. The red-and-black combination conveys intrigue and professionalism. The exterior tin has great crush resistance and allows for multiple items to be placed safely and securely within.

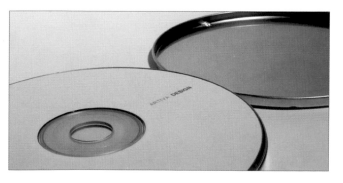

RUSH

Art Director: Dan Hoy
Designer: Savio Alphonso

Associative Color Response:
- white: cleanliness, purity, clean, sterling
- high-chroma red: brilliant, intense, energizing
- silver: cool, expensive

Appetite Rating:
- white: excellent
- high-chroma red: excellent
- silver: excellent

Associative Taste:
- high-chroma red: very sweet

Color Scheme: one hue plus neutral, white, and silver

The Rush energy drink uses unique symbolism combined with an excellent color palette to create impact on the shelf. In this case, the symbolism is metaphorically derived and uses objects that have or create/generate some type of energy, shock, or explosion.

VIVR

Art Director/Designer: Boris Ljubicic

Associative Color Response:
- pastel pink: soft, sweet, tender, rarefied, cute, comfortable, snug, delicate
- high-chroma purple: deep, power, nostalgia, memories, spirituality

Color Scheme: two points of a triad plus neutral

The Vivr product is an excellent example of color sampling. In other words, the hue of the type is being sampled from the graphic being used. The white hue of the spray cans creates a neutral background in which the typography and graphics pop.

MACNEILL GROUP

Studio: Gouthier Design: a brand collective
Creative Director: Jonathan Gouthier
Designers: Gouthier Design Creative Team

Associative Color Response:
- high-chroma blue: electric, energetic, vibrant, happy, dramatic
- blue-green: expensive, regal, classic, powerful
- neutral gray: classic, corporate

Appetite Rating:
- high-chroma blue: poor to good
- blue-green: excellent
- neutral gray: poor to good

Color Scheme: analogous with neutral gray

This small case of M&Ms was the perfect gift to launch the new brand identity within the company. The two custom blue colors allowed the brand to start making an impact on the employees and their belief in the company. The cyan, blue, and turquoise hues convey a pristine and lively work environment.

MINT CONFECTION

Art Director: John T. Drew
Designer: Kristine Yan

Associative Color Response:
• pastel green: empathy, innate, complete, soothing, natural
• earth tone: delicious, deep, rich, warm

Appetite Rating:
• pastel green: excellent
• earth tone: excellent

Associative Taste:
• no associative tastes

Color Scheme: direct complementary with shading

Mint Confection is a wonderfully executed tin with accompanying bag. Designed for a high-end market, three layers of material are utilized (cloth bow, paper wrapper, and metal tin) to contain the product. Once the tin is open, two more layers of material separate the product—chocolate mints—from the consumer. This ritual of opening, or peeling away, the layers makes the chocolates seen semiprecious and well worth the money spent.

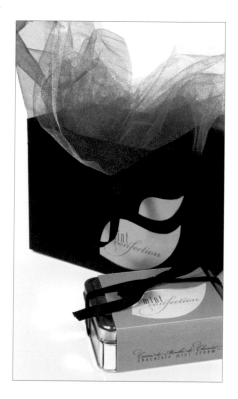

CONFECTION BREATH MINTS

Art Director: John T. Drew
Designer: Kristine Yan

Associative Color Response:
• high-chroma bluish-green: pristine, cool, fresh, liquid, refreshing, healing, wholesome

Appetite Rating:
• high-chroma bluish-green: excellent

Associative Taste:
• no associative tastes

Color Scheme: analogous with tinting

A sister product to Mint Confection, left, the same layering strategy was employed with the packaging. However, due to the complexity of the product/package design, the color palette was restrained to a simple analogous color scheme. Turquoise hues were chosen because of their color association with mint, thus conveying a pristine and refreshing package and taste.

EGEKILDE

Studio: 3PART designteam

Associative Color Response:
- pastel blue: pleasure, peace, calm, quiet, hygienic, peaceful, refreshing, clean, cool, water
- dark blue: classic, conservative, strong, dependable

Appetite Rating:
- pastel blue: excellent
- dark blue: excellent

Associative Taste:
- no associative tastes
- Dark blue: no associative taste

Color Scheme: monochromatic with tinting

This beautiful design incorporates a simple, but appropriate color scheme and an elegant form in the shape of a water drop. Color and form combine to reinforce product branding and identification.

PURIA

Art Director/Designer: Chen Wang

Associative Color Response:
- neutral gray: quality, quiet, classic
- black: powerful, elegant, spatial, mysterious

Appetite Rating:
- neutral gray: poor to good
- black: excellent

Associative Taste:
- no associative tastes

Color Scheme: achromatic

An achromatic color palette can be quite powerful. Simplistic in its construction, this type of color palette harmonizes well with the typography and bottle design.

NEW ENGLAND CRANBERRY

Studio: Bohoy Design
Art Director /Designer/Illustrator:
Johanna Bohoy

Associative Color Response:

- high-chroma red: brilliant, intense, energizing, joy, fun, aggressive
- dark-red family: rich, elegant, earthy, refined, taste, expensive, mature
- high-chroma green: ebbing of life, springtime, infancy
- dark green: natural, mature growth

Appetite Rating:

- high-chroma red: excellent

- high-chroma green: excellent
- dark green: good

Associative Taste:

- high-chroma red: very sweet

Color Scheme: complementary primaries with shading

A logo redesign for this line resulted in a new identity for placement in higher-end specialty food markets. The client wanted a clean, simple, contemporary style, distinct from the "country" look of most cranberry products. The graduated sage-green label gives it a sophisticated look.

THE FINE CHEESE CO. ENGLISH FRUITS

Studio: Irving
Designer/Illustrator: Julian Roberts

Associative Color Response:

- high-chroma red: brilliant, intense, energizing
- earth tone: delicious, deep, rich, warm
- high-chroma blue: relaxed, mature, classy, expensive
- high-chroma green-yellow: new growth, lemony, tart, fruity

Appetite Rating:

- high-chroma red: excellent

- earth tone: excellent
- high-chroma blue: poor to good
- high-chroma green-yellow: excellent

Associative Taste:

- high-chroma red: very sweet

Color Scheme: *Lime & Chilli*: two points of a triad; *Quince*: one hue plus neutral and tinting

An unusual shape and color combination for this type of product, it explodes off the shelf. This clean and simple design uses type as image to create a greater viewing distance for the consumer.

EVIAN

Studio: Curiosity
Creative Director/Designer:
Gwenazi Nicilas

Associative Color Response:

- dark blue: serene, quiet, authoritative, credible, devotion, security, service, nautical
- pastel blue: pleasure, peace, calm, quiet, hygienic, peaceful, refreshing, clean, cool, water

Appetite Rating:

- dark blue: excellent
- pastel blue: excellent

Associative Taste:

- no associative tastes

Color Scheme: monochromatic

When dealing with bottle packaging, the form of the container should be of paramount concern. There is no finer example than the Evian 2004 design, which is truly a remarkable piece, both formally and conceptually. Note how the color scheme and the shape of the bottle act as one to create a water droplet.

OPIUM

Studio: Curiosity
Creative Director/Designer:
Gwenazi Nicilas

Associative Color Response:

- earth-tone red: earthy, warm, wholesome, welcome, good, healthy, fit, sound
- yellow-orange: enterprise, drive, target, goal, luxuriance, cheer, joy, fun, excitement, stimulating

Associative Taste:

- yellow-orange: very sweet

Color Scheme: two points of a tetrad

For a successful bottling project the shape is critical—it helps to convey the tone and mood. Visual signifiers carry forth messages, and these can be broken down into three categories—form/silhouette, color, and tone/texture. Form/silhouette is the most commonly used primary signifier for any visual message, and in bottle packaging it is the most powerful.

AMARAL WINES

Studio: Estudio Iuvaro
Art Director: Cecilia Iuvaro
Designers: Mariano Gioia,
Sebastián Yáñez

Associative Color Response:

- black: winter, percussion, spatial, powerful, elegant, mysterious
- mid-green: classic

Appetite Rating:

- black: excellent
- mid-green: excellent

Associative Taste:

- no associative tastes

Color Scheme: one hue plus neutral

Viña MontGras Winery is located near the coast in the Valle de San Antonio, Leyda, in Chile. This unique maritime climate gives the Viña Amaral white wine its unique taste, therefore the simple labeling system references the kinetic movements of the ocean. Note how the blind emboss and foil stamping give the labeling system a more sophisticated, subtle approach.

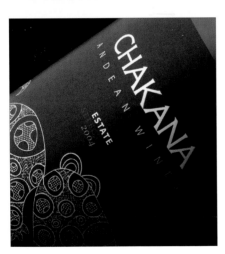

CHAKANA ANDEAN WINES

Studio: Zemma & Ruiz Moreno
Designers: Santiago Zemma,
Lucila Marina Ruiz Moreno

Associative Color Response:

- high-chroma red: dramatic, stimulating, brilliant, intense, energizing, sexy
- black: winter, percussion, spatial, powerful, elegant, mysterious
- white: cleanliness, purity, clean, sterling, innocent, perfect balance, zeal, bright, pleasure

Appetite Rating:

- high-chroma red: excellent
- black: excellent
- white: excellent

Associative Taste:

- high-chroma red: very sweet

Color Scheme: one hue plus neutral and white

The jaguar was used on this label to provide intrigue. According to one Mayan myth, the jaguar is "Lord of starry nights," and this largely black label is an excellent choice to reinforce the concept, with red used very selectively in order not to oversweeten the design.

44° NORTH VODKA

Studio: Wallace Church, Inc.
Creative Director: Stan Church
Designer: Camilla Kristiansen

Associative Color Response:
- high-chroma red: brilliant, intense, energizing, sexy, dramatic, active, stimulating, fervid, cheer, joy, fun
- dark blue: serene, quiet, authoritative, credible, devotion, security, service
- neutral gray: quality, quiet, classic, inertia, ashes, passion, practical, timeless, old age

Appetite Rating:
- high-chroma red: excellent
- dark blue: excellent
- neutral gray: poor to good

Associative Taste:
- high-chroma red: very sweet

Color Scheme: two points of a triad

The 44° North Vodka design is clean and tastefully done. The degree of latitude references the state of Idaho in the USA where the spirit is made, and the dark blue references the cool Rocky Mountain waters used in the distilling process.

ACEITES VARIETALES FAMILIA ZUCCARDI

Studio: Estudio Iuvaro
Art Director: Cecilia Iuvaro
Designers: Mariano Gioia, Sebastián Yáñez

Associative Color Response:
- dark green: nature, mountains, lakes, natural, mature growth, trustworthy, ingenuity
- mid-green: classic

Appetite Rating:
- dark green: good
- mid-green: excellent

Associative Taste:
- no associative tastes

Color Scheme: monochromatic

A color-coding system to indicate different blends of olive oils is created through a combination of different ink values of green and colored substrates.

CAVES VIDIGAL

Studio: estudiocrop
Art Director: Dado Queiroz
Designers: Dado Queiroz, Renan Molin
Photographer: Fabiano Schroden

Associative Color Response:
- dark red: rich, elegant, refined, taste, expensive, mature
- mid-range orange: gentle, entice, good spirits

Appetite Rating:
- mid-range orange: good to excellent

Associative Taste:
- mid-range orange: sweet

Color Scheme: two points of a near complementary with shading and tinting

The Caves Vidigal label is an excellent example of harmony through color and line. This is achieved in the color palette through yellow and magenta; whereas, through line, harmony is achieved by the line vernacular within all parts of the type and graphics.

ETCHED TURKEY THANKSGIVING WINE (2004)

Studio: Wallace Church, Inc.
Creative Director: Stan Church
Designer: Akira Yasuda

Associative Color Response:
• black: powerful, elegant, mysterious, spatial
• white: refreshing, perfect balance, zeal, bright

Appetite Rating:
• black: excellent
• white: excellent

Associative Taste:
• no associative tastes

Color Scheme: direct complementary

The 2004 Thanksgiving wine-bottle design is masterfully executed through harmony and complementary colors. The black is reinforced through the color of the glass and the neck label, whereas white is used to make the mark pop off the bottle.

VALLE ESCONDIDO WINERY

Studio: Estudio Iuvaro
Art Director: Cecilia Iuvaro
Designers: Mariano Gioia, Sebastián Yáñez

Associative Color Response:
• dark gray: cultured, professional, wise, classic, expensive, sophisticated
• pastel blue: pleasure, peace, calm, quiet, clean, cool, water, hygienic, peaceful, refreshing, heavenly

Appetite Rating:
• dark gray: excellent
• pastel blue: excellent

Associative Taste:
• no associative tastes

Color Scheme: one hue with tinting and shading

Color is used in a twofold manner within this labeling system. Each variety of wine has a distinctive color palette to differentiate itself from the other wines under the same label, and to distinguish which wine is best for which season. A blind emboss is used to help create kinetic energy and continuity within the illustration across the system.

LAS PERDICES RANGE

Studio: Estudio Iuvaro
Art Director: Cecilia Iuvaro
Designers: Mariano Gioia, Sebastián Yáñez

Associative Color Response:
• dark orange: exhilarating, inspiring, stirring, stimulating, moving, provoking, most exciting
• earth-tone red: warmhearted, welcome, good, healthy, fit, sound
• high-chroma pink: stimulates, aggressive, genial, exciting, happy, high, fun, excitement, sensual, cheer, joy

Appetite Rating:
• high-chroma pink: excellent

Associative Taste:
• high-chroma pink: very sweet

Color Scheme: one hue plus neutral

The use of color as a branding vehicle differentiates the variety of wines under the same label. Copper-foil stamping and a blind emboss create further visual separation within a labeling system that creates its own vernacular.

SEPTIMA ROSÉ WINE

Studio: Zemma & Ruiz Moreno
Designers: Santiago Zemma,
Lucila Marina Ruiz Moreno

Associative Color Response:
- dark orange: exhilarating, inspiring, stirring, stimulating, moving, provoking
- mid-range pink-red: restrained, toned down, soft, subdued, quiet
- black: elegant, classic

Appetite Rating:
- mid-range pink-red: good
- black: excellent

Associative Taste:
- mid-range pink-red: sweet

Color Scheme: one hue plus neutral with shading

The color of the wine plays the dominant role in establishing the color palette here, and each hue in the label works in concert with it. The white labels suggest purity and freshness and function well on a clear bottle that does not alter the natural hue of the wine.

PAZZO

Creative Director: David Schwemann

Associative Color Response:
- high-chroma red: brilliant, intense, energizing, sexy, dramatic, stimulating
- high-chroma yellow: agreeable, pleasant, welcome, vigorous, noble, youthful energy
- black: powerful, elegant, mysterious, spatial

Appetite Rating:
- high-chroma red: excellent
- high-chroma yellow: good
- black: excellent

Associative Taste:
- high-chroma red: very sweet
- high-chroma yellow: very sweet

Color Scheme: two points of a tetrad plus neutral

This unusual labeling system is highly kinetic through its use of color, form, and line. Superbly done, the Pazzo graphics are a visual feast.

RED ROVER

Creative Director: David Schwemann

Associative Color Response:
- high-chroma red: brilliant, intense, energizing, sexy, dramatic, stimulating
- high-chroma orange: cleanliness, producing, healing, tasty, growing
- black: powerful, elegant, mysterious, spatial

Appetite Rating:
- high-chroma red: excellent
- high-chroma orange: excellent
- black: excellent

Associative Taste:
- high-chroma red: very sweet
- high-chroma orange: very sweet

Color Scheme: two points of a split complementary plus neutral

The simplistic color palette in combination with the typography and illustration create a unique labeling system. The symmetrical arrangement of type and image creates a strong focal point in conjunction with the bold-red neck label and high-chroma orange label, making this design explode visually off the shelf.

Three Colors

Three-color package design is a rare category of work. It is true that three-color work is less expensive than four-color, however, the cost benefit these days is negligible, so why is three-color work still undertaken? Three-color package design falls in line with one- and two-color jobs. To create high-end design, a mastery of color, shape, imagery, typography, concept, and composition is required. When these parts do not work together, the package design will appear cheap and inexpensive.

Any three-color job—logo, annual report, brochure, T-shirt design, or package design—creates hue flexibility. For example, cyan, magenta, and yellow create all the different high-chroma hues found within the 12-step color wheel. With the added technique of overprinting, a solid understanding of color theory, and a pragmatic understanding of ink opacity and hue mixing, three-color design can create a striking impact. Couple hue flexibility with the behavioral effects of color, and you have the most powerful tool available to designers. There is no doubt about it—color sells your product.

PADDYWAX DESTINATIONS

Studio: Principle
Art Director: Pamela Zuccker
Designer: Jennifer Sukis
Photographer: Kara Brennan © 2007

Associative Color Response:
• brown: calm, pleasing, rich, thought-provoking, serenity
• orange: warm, cleanliness, joy, happy

Color Scheme: simple analogous with shading

This wonderfully executed package design uses color to convey a cohesive whole across the overall system and uses hue to signify the individual fragrances within it. Sparing no expense, the materials used coupled with the overall design strategy signifies quality and imbues consumer confidence.

PADDYWAX JOLIE

Studio: Principle
Art Director: Pamela Zuccker
Designer: Ally Gerson
Photographer: Kara Brennan © 2007

Associative Color Response:
• pastel green: completely, calm, quiet, smoothing, natural
• green-yellow: new growth
• high-chroma pink: stimulates, aggressive, genial, exciting, happy

Color Scheme: complementary with tinting

Color sells your product, and there is no finer example than this package design. Complementary colors with tinting are used for each variety, creating a highly kinetic design. Pattern is used to create stability and continuity within the system.

RASTA MIND INTERNATIONAL

Studio: estudiocrop
Art Director/Designer: Dado Queiroz
Photographer: Fabiano Schroden

Associative Color Response:
- high-chroma red: brilliant,
  sexy, intense, energizing,
  dramatic, stimulating
- black: powerful, elegant, mysterious,
  heavy, basic
- white: cleanliness, purity,
  clean, sterling

Color Scheme: one hue with white and black

This package is a simple, elegant, and clean design, in which texture is used as a visual magnet within the typography. The anatomical structure of the typography is well chosen, the width-to-height ratio is proportionate to the format of the box, thus creating harmony.

BABU

Art Director/Designer: Chris Walden

Associative Color Response:
- mid-range pink-red: restrained,
  toned down, soft
- mid-green: classic
- high-chroma blue: spaciousness, dignity,
  cool, electric, energetic

Appetite Rating:
- mid-range pink-red: good
- mid-green: excellent
- high-chroma blue: poor to good

Associative Taste:
- mid-range pink-red: sweet

Color Scheme: analogous with tinting, shading, and black

This is an excellent example of a simple analogous color palette with tinting and shading. Black is used to give the color palette density and visual separation. White,

in this case, is the color of the substrate and would be considered a hue within the color palette, but would create no additional cost when printing. The design is an excellent color study for examining the legibility of type when reversed out to the substrate.

CHOKLAD PLÄTTS

Studio: dododesign.se
Art Director/Designer: Dejan Mauzer

Associative Color Response:
- dark red: rich, elegant, refined, taste, expensive, mature, earthy
- high-chroma yellow-orange: fun, enterprise, drive, target, goal, luxuriance, cheer, joy, excitement
- high-chroma red: brilliant, intense, energizing

Appetite Rating:
- dark red: poor
- high-chroma yellow-orange: excellent
- high-chroma red: excellent

Associative Taste:
- high-chroma yellow-orange: very sweet
- high-chroma red: very sweet

Color Scheme: analogous with tinting and shading

The playful use of the typography coupled with the vibrant colors creates a highly dynamic composition. The muted dark red allows the high-chroma yellow and orange to pop on the box, creating a three-dimensional illusion on a two-dimensional plane. The swirls and the background converge underneath the focal point of the composition to lift the name off the page.

AROMAFLORIA

Art Director: Tanya Quick
Designer: Fernando Munoz

Associative Color Response:
- mid-range pink-red: restrained, toned down, soft, subdued, quiet
- high-chroma orange: healing, tasty, growing, fire, warm, cleanliness, cheerfulness
- high-chroma green: life, use, springtime, infancy, motion, ebbing of life

Color Scheme: Analogous with tinting, shading, and black

The AromaFloria package design series is wonderfully executed, using a multitude of substrates, including plastic, glass, tin, paper, and wood. The color scheme unifies the design and the different substrates, while also color coding all the components. Note: A die cut is used so that the wooden stick can act as a lock for the paper packaging.

KING DELIGHT

Creative Director: Micha Goes
Designer: Andi Friedl

Associative Color Response:
- high-chroma orange: healing, tasty, warm, cleanliness, cheerfulness
- high-chroma green-yellow: new growth, lemony, tart, fruity

Appetite Rating:
- high-chroma orange: excellent
- high-chroma green-yellow: excellent

Associative Taste:
- high-chroma orange: very sweet

Color Scheme: two points of a triad

Going against color conventions, the King Delight package design won the 2004 Food Service Award, despite using a high-chroma greenish-yellow hue that is not generally considered appropriate for meat products. However, the color is not juxtaposed with the product, therefore no unwanted psychological effects occur—a brilliant strategy to use the psychological and learned behavioral properties of the hue without incurring any of the negatives associated with it.

ARLA MAELK

Designer: Jens Dreier

Associative Color Response:
- black: basic, neutral, cold, classic, strong
- white: light, cool, snow, cleanliness, purity, clean, sterling, innocent
- high-chroma green-yellow: new growth
- high-chroma bluish-purple: classic, powerful
- earth tone: delicious, deep, rich, warm, folksy
- high-chroma yellow-orange: cheer, joy, fun, excitement, stimulates

Appetite Rating:
- black: excellent
- white: excellent
- high-chroma green-yellow: excellent
- high-chroma bluish-purple: excellent
- earth tone: excellent
- high-chroma yellow-orange: excellent

Associative Taste:
- high-chroma yellow-orange: very sweet

Color Scheme: incongruous

Simple and classic color combinations are used in conjunction with a highly kinetic illustration to create impact on the shelf. White is used for whole milk, brown for chocolate milk, and a bluish-purple for low-fat milk.

LOVE GLOVE

Art Director/Designer: Chapman Tse

Associative Color Response:

- high-chroma red: surging, brilliant, intense, energizing, sexy, dramatic, stimulating, active, cheer, joy, fun
- high-chroma orange: producing, healing, tasty, growing, fire, warm, cleanliness, cheerfulness
- earth tone: rustics, delicious, deep, rich, warm, folksy, rooted, life

Color Scheme: analogous with shading

An excellent example of a simple analogous color palette with shading, the Love Glove package design is beautifully executed. The shutter top with die-cut sides allows the consumer to preview the product. With an inner box (shown top), the rigidity for crush resistance is improved during shipping.

THE POSSUM TROT ORCHESTRA

Studio: One Lucky Guitar, Inc.
Art Directors: Matt Kelley, John Minton

Associative Color Response:

- pastel blue: pleasure, calm, quiet, hygienic, peaceful, refreshing
- white: purity, clean, sterling, innocent, silent, inexplicable, normality, life, work, school
- dark orange: exhilarating, passive, inspiring, stirring, stimulating, moving, provoking, most exciting,

Color Scheme: near complementary with shading

This near complementary palette is a wonderful example of a push-pull technique when expanding unique color palettes. The pastel blue is shaded to darken the hue slightly and, in this case, pull it forward. The red-orange has a large amount of shading combined with tinting to push the hue back. Generally, cool colors recede and warm colors come forward. However, the effect of colors depends on their context, and in this unusual color combination, the norm is reversed.

SEE'S CANDY

Art Director: John T. Drew
Designer: Sachi Ito

Associative Color Response:
- high-chroma yellow-orange: fun, enterprise, drive, target, goal, luxuriance, cheer, joy, excitement
- high-chroma red: brilliant, intense, energizing, sexy, dramatic, stimulating
- black: powerful, elegant, mysterious, heavy, basic, neutral

Appetite Rating:
- high-chroma yellow-orange: excellent
- high-chroma red: excellent
- black: excellent

Associative Taste:
- high-chroma yellow-orange: very sweet
- high-chroma red: very sweet

Color Scheme: two points of a tetrad plus neutral

By adding a thread to the exterior of the package design, a tactile experience is created. The more senses involved in opening a package design, the more memorable the design will be.

HOW TO MAKE YOUR OWN CANDLE

Art Director: Mary Ann McLaughlin
Designer: Mashael Al Sulaiti

Associative Color Response:
- high-chroma red: brilliant, intense, energizing, sexy, dramatic, stimulating
- black: powerful, elegant, mysterious, heavy, basic, neutral
- high-chroma orange: producing, healing, tasty, growing, fire, warm, cleanliness, cheerfulness, masculine
- blue-green: pristine, cleanliness, pure, serious

Color Scheme: one hue plus neutral

The substrate is primarily an orange hue that has been tinted and shaded to an earth-tone red, creating a near analogous color palette with the red and orange hues with which it harmonizes well. The turquoise is a near complementary color palette with the substrate.

DROOBLES BUBBLE GUM

Art Director: John T. Drew
Designer: Rachel Pearson

Associative Color Response:
- pastel blue: refreshing, clean, cool, water
- dark blue: basic, confident, classic, strong
- high-chroma blue: height, lively, pleasing, rich

Appetite Rating:
- pastel blue: good
- dark blue: excellent
- high-chroma blue: poor to good

Associative Taste:
- no associative tastes

Color Scheme: monochromatic

This simple, but eloquently conceived monochromatic study is refreshingly reinforced through the typographic specimen chosen, texture, and line work.

FOCUS

Studio: Mostardesign Studio
Art Director/Designer: Olivier Gourvat

Associative Color Response:
- high-chroma red: surging, brilliant, intense, energizing, sexy, dramatic, stimulating
- white: purity, clean, sterling, innocent, silent, inexplicable, normality, life, work, school
- bluish-purple: powerful, regal, classic

Color Scheme: two points of a tetrad with white

Intensely beautiful, the Mostardesign Focus packaging consists of 15 illustrations generated by the studio as a self-promotional piece. A plastic red Mylar, duplex, and a high-chroma white cover-weight paper is used to help expand the color palette and to frame the work.

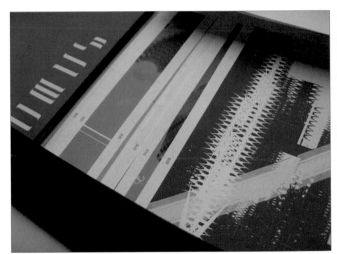

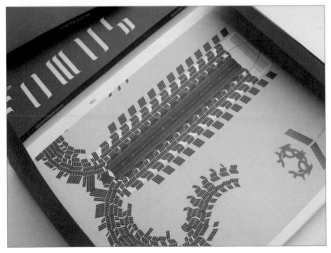

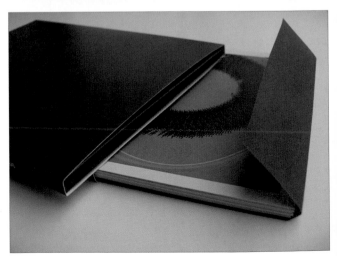

POPHAUS TYPE FOUNDRY

Art Director: John T. Drew
Designer: Lydia Adi

Associative Color Response:

- high-chroma red: excitability, solid, aggression, provocative, strength
- high-chroma yellow: agreeable, pleasant, welcome, vigorous, noble, youthful energy, speed, movement
- high-chroma blue: sobriety, calm, height, lively, pleasing, rich, levels, vertical, honesty, strength, work

Color Scheme: primaries

A self-promotional piece, the Pophaus Type Foundry buttons and the companion palm brochure—a nonfolding brochure that fits in the hand—are wonderfully conceived. Here, the information on the brochure is printed on the back, and the buttons are held in place by inserting the needle through the palm brochure.

AVON PLANET SPA

Art Director: Tanya Quick
Designer: Fernando Munoz

Associative Color Response:

- earth-tone orange: earthy, warm, wholesome, welcome, good, healthy, fit, sound
- black: winter, percussion, spatial, powerful, elegant, mysterious

Color Scheme: monochromatic plus neutral

This series is an interesting example of both a monochromatic study and a simple analogous color palette. A white varnish is applied to the bottles and tubes to give it a sand-blasted-glass feel. A monochromatic and simple analogous color palette will always harmonize, making for a restful experience.

DEEP HERBAL

Studio: Fuelhaus
Art Director: Kellie Schroeder
Designer: Ty Webb

Associative Color Response:

- dark red: rich, elegant, refined, taste, expensive, mature, earthy, strong
- dark green: nature, mountains, lakes, natural, mature growth, versatility, traditional
- white: inexplicable, normality, work

Color Scheme: direct complementary with shading

This design is a great example of how to use the same hues in different arrangements to create multiple color studies. By using different proportions of colors and placement, the same hue palette can potentially be used for a range of products, branding the product through color, but achieving diversity through proportion and placement.

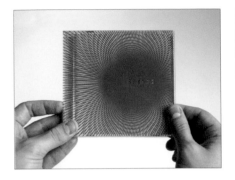
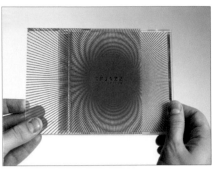
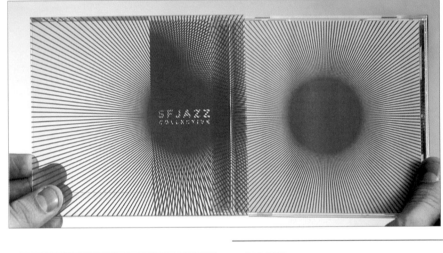

SF JAZZ COLLECTIVE

Studio: Doyle Partners

Associative Color Response:

- high-chroma pink: stimulates, aggressive, genial, exciting, happy, high, fun, excitement, attention-getting
- high-chroma yellow-green: lemony, tart, fruity, acidic, sharp, bold, trendy, strength, sunlight, biology
- high-chroma bluish-purple: regal, classic, expensive, powerful, tender, longing, elegant, mystical, spiritual

Color Scheme: primary and two secondaries (incongruous)

The SF Jazz Collective is directed by Joshua Redman and features legendary vibes-player Bobby Hutcherson. For this live recording, the goal was to package the excitement of the performance without appearing to be a traditional jazz album. Two hundred straight lines are arranged in a spiral and printed on a translucent cover and then again on the booklet inside. By sliding the jewel case out of the cover, a lively psychedelic effect is created.

VAGABOND

Studio: CF NAPA
Creative Director: David Schwemann

Associative Color Response:

- high-chroma red: surging, brilliant, intense, energizing, sexy, dramatic, stimulating, fervid, active, cheer, joy, fun, aggressive
- high-chroma orange: producing, healing, tasty, growing, fire, warm, cleanliness, cheerfulness, masculine
- high-chroma yellow-orange: enterprise, drive, target, goal, luxuriance, cheer, fun, joy, excitement, stimulates, aggressive, powerful
- black: percussion, spatial, powerful, elegant, mysterious

Appetite Rating:

- high-chroma red: excellent
- high-chroma orange: excellent
- high-chroma yellow-orange: excellent
- black: excellent

Associative Taste:

- high-chroma red: very sweet
- high-chroma orange: very sweet
- high-chroma yellow-orange: very sweet

Color Scheme: analogous plus black

The warm analogous color palette pops off the black glass. Note how the black outlines within the illustration tie into the color of the bottle and neck label.

EPONA

Studio: Alian Design
Art Director/Designer: Ian Shimkoviak

Associative Color Response:

- high-chroma orange: producing, healing, tasty, growing, fire, warm, cleanliness, cheerfulness, masculine
- high-chroma yellow-orange: enterprise, drive, target, goal, luxuriance, cheer, joy, fun, excitement, stimulates, aggressive, powerful, energy
- high-chroma blue: dignity, spaciousness, sobriety, calm, height, lively, pleasing, rich

Color Scheme: direct complementary

This is an awesome example of using color to promote shelf recognition. The direct color complementary color palette uses a warm and cool color scheme making the labeling system explode off the bottle. The analogous color palettes in a number of the labels are tinted less than 40 percent of their opacity to create a dramatic contrast differential from the bottle.

KEY

Studio: Deser
Art Director/Designer: M. Piotrowski

Associative Color Response:

- high-chroma blue: dignity, spaciousness, sobriety, calm, height, lively, pleasing, rich
- silver: futuristic, cool, expensive, money, valuable, classic
- high-chroma yellow: friendly, hot, luminous, energy, magnanimity, intuition, intellect, loudest, brightest, young

Color Scheme: primaries plus neutral

This underwear packaging is a great example of using two different types of substrate to achieve the visual impact desired. Printed graphics on paper are inserted into a clear plastic tube to achieve high-quality graphics and to emulate a third type of substrate—a metal container.

FRANCK

Studio: Design B
Art Director/Designer: Boris Ljubicic
Photographers/Illustrators:
Boris Ljubicic, Igor Masnjak

Associative Color Response:
- high-chroma red: surging, brilliant, intense, energizing, sexy, dramatic, stimulating, fervid, active, cheer, joy, fun

- dark green: nature, mountains, lakes, natural, mature growth, versatility, traditional, money, trustworthy, refreshing
- gold: warm, opulent, expensive, radiant, valuable, prestigious

Appetite Rating:
- high-chroma red: excellent
- dark green: good
- gold: excellent

Associative Taste:
- high-chroma red: very sweet

Color Scheme: direct complementary with shading plus white

This package design is a wonderful example of a direct complementary color palette being used to create diversity within a product line. Three hues (dark green, red, and gold) are proportionately changed to create brand recognition for each product within the line.

PERLA

Studio: DESer
Art Director/Designer: M. Piotrowski

Associative Color Response:
- high-chroma red: surging, sexy, brilliant, intense, energizing, dramatic, stimulating
- high-chroma green: life, use, motion, ebbing of life, springtime, infancy, wilderness, fresh
- gold: warm, opulent, expensive, radiant, valuable, prestigious

Appetite Rating:
- high-chroma red: excellent
- high-chroma green: excellent
- gold: excellent

Associative Taste:
- high-chroma red: very sweet

Color Scheme: direct complementary with gold

The direct complementary color palette used here conveys an organic feel, and the line work found within the graphics is reminiscent of farm fields. The red shield and band pop off the cooler green background allowing for ease of readability and brand recognition.

BRIANNAS

Studio: The Hively Agency
Art Director/Designer: Sarah Munt

Associative Color Response:
- black: powerful, elegant, mysterious, classic
- earth tone: rustics, delicious, deep, rich, warm, folksy, rooted, life, work, wholesome
- high-chroma orange: healing, tasty, growing, fire, warm, cleanliness, cheerfulness
- dark red: rich, elegant, refined, taste, expensive, mature, earthy, strong, warm, ripe
- high-chroma reddish-purple: sweet taste, subtle, tender longing, romanticism, exciting, sensual
- mid-green: nature, mountains, lakes, natural, mature growth, versatility, traditional

Appetite Rating:
- black: excellent
- earth tone: good
- high-chroma orange: excellent
- high-chroma reddish-purple: excellent
- mid-green: good

Associative Taste:
- high-chroma orange: very sweet

Color Scheme: two points of a split complementary with shading

The symmetrical balance, typographic arrangement, and color scheme stays consistent with the typographical arrangement, allowing for greater flexibility within the illustrations. Each illustration creates a strong focal point to promote shelf recognition.

RIGHT GUARD

Studio: Wallace Church, Inc.
Creative Director: Stan Church
Designer: John Bruno

Associative Color Response:
- dark blue: serene, quiet, authoritative, credible, devotion, security, service
- high-chroma yellow: agreeable, pleasant, welcome, vigorous, noble, youthful energy, speed, movement
- high-chroma yellow-green: lemony, tart, fruity, acidic, sharp, bold, trendy, strength, sunlight, biology
- high-chroma blue: dignity, spaciousness, sobriety, calm, height, lively, pleasing, rich
- high-chroma reddish-purple: sweet taste, subtle, restlessness, prolongs life, feminine elegance, tender longing, romanticism

Color Scheme: Incongruous

Gillette enlisted Wallace Church to help refresh the brand's True Blue essence and more effectively target both core brand users and the new Xtreme consumer. The communication hierarchy and composition was optimized to better promote the energized Right Guard brandmark. Textured backgrounds and updated icons were incorporated to communicate a contemporary masculine image, while Xtreme's glowing X was amplified to signal a more youthful experience.

WASP

Studio: design@qirk.com
Designer: Daryl Geary

Associative Color Response:
- high-chroma orange: cheerful, lively, exciting, bright, luminous, tasty, growing, fire, warm, cleanliness, cheerfulness
- high-chroma yellow-green: lemony, tart, fruity, acidic, sharp, bold, trendy, strength, sunlight, biology
- high-chroma reddish-purple: subtle, sweet taste, exciting, sensual
- high-chroma blue: height, lively, pleasing, rich, cold, wet

Appetite Rating:
- high-chroma orange: excellent
- high-chroma yellow-green: excellent
- high-chroma reddish-purple: excellent
- high-chroma blue: good

Associative Taste:
- high-chroma orange: very sweet
- high-chroma yellow-green: very sweet, lemony

Color Scheme: tetrad

A true high-chroma tetrad, the Wasp Energy Drink utilizes brand recognition through color in a masterful way. Note how the hues are even injected into the drink itself, branding the product without the need for graphics or typography.

U'LUVKA

Studio: Aloof Design
Art Director: Sam Aloof
Designer: Andrew Scrase,
Jon Hodkinson

Associative Color Response:
• silver: futuristic, cool, expensive, money, valuable, classic
• black: winter, percussion, spatial, powerful, elegant, mysterious, heavy, basic
• earth tone: deep, rich, warm, durable, secure

Appetite Rating:
• black: excellent
• silver: excellent
• earth tone: excellent

Associative Taste:
• no associative tastes

Color Scheme: near achromatic

U'luvka Vodka is an exceptional package system for the luxury market. Black, brown, silver, and a spot varnish create a unique color scheme that is delicately executed. The unique bottle designs and custom packaging create an air of quality that is unsurpassed within this marketplace, making U'luvka Vodka an extremely successful branding strategy.

MOSSBACK

Studio: CF NAPA
Creative Director: David Schwemann

Associative Color Response:
- gold: warm, opulent, expensive, radiant, valuable, prestigious
- high-chroma red: surging, brilliant, intense, energizing, sexy, dramatic, stimulating
- high-chroma yellow-orange: enterprise, drive, target, goal, luxuriance, cheer, joy, fun, excitement, stimulates
- high-chroma orange: producing, healing, tasty, growing, fire, warm, cleanliness, cheerfulness, masculine, fearlessness, curiosity

Appetite Rating:
- gold: excellent
- high-chroma red: excellent
- high-chroma yellow-orange: excellent
- high-chroma orange: excellent

Associative Taste:
- high-chroma red: very sweet
- high-chroma yellow-orange: very sweet
- high-chroma orange: very sweet

Color Scheme: complex analogous with shading plus neutral

UV ink is used on the label to create texture and depth. The natural color of the wine combined with the dark-green bottle creates the hue black that harmonizes perfectly with the labeling system.

TURNING LEAVES

Studio: Wallace Church, Inc.
Creative Director: Stan Church
Designer: Nin Glaister

Associative Color Response:
- high-chroma yellow-orange: enterprise, drive, target, goal, luxuriance, cheer, joy, fun, excitement, stimulates
- high-chroma orange: producing, healing, tasty, growing, fire, warm, cleanliness, cheerfulness
- dark-red family: rich, elegant, refined, taste, expensive, mature
- high-chroma red: surging, sexy, brilliant, intense, energizing, dramatic, stimulating

Appetite Rating:
- high-chroma yellow-orange: excellent
- high-chroma orange: excellent
- high-chroma red: excellent

Associative Taste:
- high-chroma yellow-orange: very sweet
- high-chroma orange: very sweet
- high-chroma red: very sweet

Color Scheme: analogous plus black

This complex analogous color scheme is beautifully executed on black glass to create an incredible design. Note how the label wraps around each bottle, working on a micro level, and when placed together the label works on a macro level by creating a much larger labeling system for viewing at a distance.

CAPTAIN MORGAN PRIVATE STOCK

Studio: SandorMax
Designer: Zoltan Csillag

Associative Color Response:
- high-chroma yellow-orange: enterprise, drive, target, goal, luxuriance, cheer, joy, fun, excitement, stimulates
- high-chroma red: brilliant, intense, energizing, sexy, dramatic, stimulating
- black: winter, percussion, spatial, powerful, elegant, mysterious

Appetite Rating:
- high-chroma yellow-orange: excellent
- high-chroma red: excellent
- black: excellent

Associative Taste:
- high-chroma yellow-orange: very sweet
- high-chroma red: very sweet

Color Scheme: analogous with shading plus a black hue

Concept designs for the launch of Captain Morgan's Premium Rum, Private Stock. Note how sampling the color of the rum creates the foundation of the color palette.

BE FRIENDS

Studio: Zemma & Ruiz Moreno

Associative Color Response:
- gold: warm, opulent, expensive, radiant, valuable, prestigious
- earth tone: deep, rich, warm
- black: winter, percussion, spatial, powerful, elegant, mysterious

Appetite Rating:
- gold: excellent
- earth tone: good
- black: excellent

Associative Taste:
- no associative tastes

Color Scheme: simple analogous plus black

The labeling system is sophisticated and elegant, conveyed through a bronze-and-gold hue. The gold honeybee is foil stamped to convey the same connotations as a crescent shield, whereas the typographic composition and font structure is clean.

SMS

Studio: International
Art Director/Designer/Photographer:
Boris Ljubicic

Associative Color Response:
- high-chroma red: surging, sexy, brilliant, intense, energizing, dramatic, stimulating
- high-chroma orange: producing, healing, tasty, growing, fire, warm, cleanliness, cheerfulness
- dark green: nature, mountains, lakes, natural, mature growth, versatility, traditional, money, trustworthy, refreshing
- silver: futuristic, cool, expensive, money, valuable, classic

Appetite Rating:
- high-chroma red: excellent
- high-chroma orange: excellent
- dark green: good
- silver: excellent

Associative Taste:
- high-chroma red: very sweet
- high-chroma orange: very sweet

Color Scheme: near analogous with a complementary green and blue

The design of the SMS olive oil bottle is rooted in the legend of how the St. Peter's Fish got its name. When St. Peter was baptizing people, he rolled up his pant legs to let some fish swim through. As they passed he noticed an unusual looking one. He reached down, grabbed the fish, and said, "You will be called the same as I." This is why the fish has one black stain on its left side and four lines on its right side—the marks of a thumb and four fingers. To represent this, the bottle has a concave imprint that operates as a unique ergonomic design. This beautifully conceived design relates culturally to the product's branding.

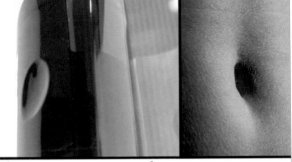

ECHOES OF SUMMER

Studio: Bohoy Design
Creative Director/Designer:
Johnanna Bohoy

Associative Color Response:
- gold: warm, opulent, expensive, radiant, valuable, prestigious
- high-chroma red: surging, hope, brilliant, intense, energizing, sexy, dramatic, stimulating, fervid, active, cheer, joy, fun, aggressive
- high-chroma yellow: anticipation, agreeable, pleasant, welcome, vigorous, noble, youthful energy

Appetite Rating:
- gold: excellent
- high-chroma red: excellent
- high-chroma yellow: good

Associative Taste:
- high-chroma red: very sweet
- high-chroma yellow: very sweet

Color Scheme: warm incongruous

A color palette that conveys the taste of summer; the Echoes of Summer fruit jams, chutneys, and fruit butters have a glowing sun behind the single fruit with a gold cap, gold bottom border, and gold type that complement yellow and red.

Four Colors

Rarely is a package design printed solely with four colors. Most often there is at least a flood varnish, making the job five colors. In many cases, a four-color process job will contain a flood varnish, spot varnish, and one or two spot hues—a Pantone, Toyo, or Trumatch hue, for example. In these cases, different color effects are used to create different levels of subtlety or visual impact, and they can create a level of sophistication unsurpassed by any other technique found within print-based graphics.

With the globalization of the marketplace and advancements in new technology, the amount of four-color package design being printed today has skyrocketed. This relatively new phenomenon has changed the way consumers view the qualitative level of the products they buy. As a designer, it has never been more important to understand color in all its forms. This includes an appreciation of the many substrates that are available to enhance the perceived value of a product and its delivery system—packaging.

ANDREW'S TIES

Art Director/Designer: Inyoung Choi

Associative Color Response:
- high-chroma red: brilliant, intense, energizing, sexy, dramatic, stimulating
- black: percussion, spatial, powerful, elegant, mysterious
- dark green: traditional, money, trustworthy, refreshing

Color Scheme: direct complementary plus neutral

The bags and tie boxes are classified as iconic packaging, and the visual communication is direct and immediate (hard sale). The other boxes and bags use color symbolism to create a soft-sale approach. Note: The hard-sale components are placed on the shelf and used as store-display items for consumer recognition; the soft-sale items are used after the merchandise has been bought to pack for safe travel.

JACQUELINE KENNEDY: THE WHITE HOUSE YEARS

Studio: Nita B. Creative
Art Director: Renita Breitenbucher
Designers: Andrea Egbert, Kimberly Welter, Renita Breitenbucher
Illustration: Virginia Johnson

Associative Color Response:
- high-chroma pink: stimulates, aggressive, genial, exciting, happy, high, fun, excitement, attention-getting, promising
- pastel pink: soft, sweet, tender, cute, comfortable, snug, rarefied, delicate, female babies, delicate, cozy, subtle
- black: spatial, powerful, elegant, mysterious, heavy, basic, neutral
- high-chroma green: life, use, motion, ebbing of life, springtime, infancy, wilderness, hope, peace

Color Scheme: direct complementary plus yellow and neutral

Marshall Field's, sponsor of "Jacqueline Kennedy: The White House Years" at the Field Museum in Chicago, wanted to capture Jackie Kennedy's sense of style for the product packaging to accompany the exhibit. From collector's plates, to fine porcelain pillboxes, to an elegant, almost aristocratic stationery set, the range is graced with classic images of the white gloves, dresses, coats, and pillbox hats that she made famous. The timeless, elegant packaging—a work of art in its own right—was designed in "Jackie pink," with cloth-covered button detailing capturing the spirit, style, and grace that she embodied. Special care was taken when considering "Jackie pink," as it was the color that would tie the branding together on the store shelves. The watercolor illustrations by Virginia Johnson incorporate a perfect array of colors to reflect the texture and style of each item of clothing.

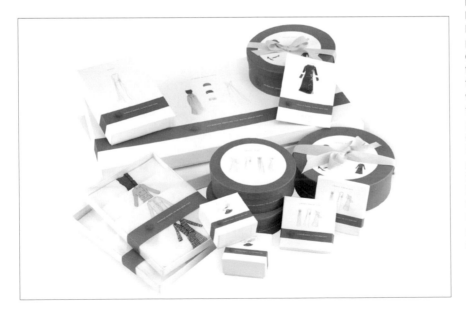

GANESH AND KRISHNA KITS

Studio: Alian Design
Art Director/Designer: Ian Shimkoviak

Associative Color Response:

- dark gray: wise, cultured, mature, professional, classic, expensive, sophisticated, solid, enduring
- neutral gray: quality, quiet, classic, inertia, ashes, passion, practical, timeless, old age, cunning, cool
- high-chroma yellow-orange: enterprise, drive, target, goal, luxuriance, cheer, joy, fun, excitement, stimulates
- dark orange: exhilarating, inspiring, stirring, stimulating, moving, provoking
- high-chroma orange: producing, healing, tasty, growing, fire, warm, cleanliness, cheerfulness
- high-chroma blue: dignity, spaciousness, sobriety, calm, height, lively, pleasing, rich
- mid-green: safari, warlike, forces, military, camouflaged, classic

Color Scheme: *Ganesh Kit* analogous with complementary *Krishna Kit* achromatic with complementary

The high quality of the materials used in the Ganesh and Krishna boxes is evident when picked up. This sense of quality is conveyed through the materials used both inside and out—a branding strategy that ultimately yields an increase in profit margin.

BELLE HOP

Studio: SGDP
Creative Director: Marcus Norman
Designers: Marcus Norman, Augusta Toppins
Illustrators: Robyn Neild, Augusta Toppins

Associative Color Response:

- black: spatial, powerful, elegant, mysterious, heavy, basic, neutral
- high-chroma red: surging, brilliant, intense, energizing, sexy, dramatic, stimulating
- high-chroma blue: dignity, spaciousness, sobriety, calm, height, lively, pleasing, rich
- earth-tone red: warm, wholesome, welcome, good, healthy, fit, sound
- high-chroma reddish-purple: sweet taste, subtle, restlessness, prolongs life, feminine elegance, tender longing

Color Scheme: two points of a triad plus neutral

This packaging was developed to appeal to women in a personal and romantic way. With travel as the central concept, the idea was embellished by using a contemporary, unique illustration to create a persona, an array of "passport-inspired" graphic elements, and a soft, neutral, feminine color palette that allowed the various bright colors of the product to speak clearly. All packages were designed wirh a consistent color palette to create a unified system, and the substrate used allowed the vivid colors to be clearly visible.

FLORA

Art Director: Kelly Bryant
Designer: Kat McCluskey

Associative Color Response:

- high-chroma red: surging, sexy, brilliant, intense, energizing, dramatic, stimulating
- earth-tone red: warm, wholesome, welcome, good, healthy, fit, sound
- high-chroma blue: dignity, spaciousness, sobriety, calm, height, lively, pleasing, rich
- high-chroma yellow-orange: enterprise, drive, target, goal, luxuriance, cheer, joy, fun, excitement, stimulates
- dark orange: exhilarating, inspiring, stirring, stimulating, moving, provoking
- hearth-tone red: warm, wholesome, welcome, good, healthy, fit, sound

Color Scheme: incongruous

The Flora package has a beautifully executed, near complementary color palette. The striped exterior helps create an exaggerated verticality.

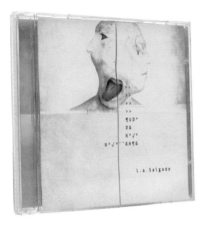

L. A. SALGADO

Studio: estudiocrop and L. A. Salgado
Art Directors: Beto Janz, Dado Queiroz
Designer: Dado Queiroz
Illustrator: Beto Janz Oswaldo S. Lima
Photographer: Fabiano Schroden

Associative Color Response:

- black: spatial, powerful, elegant, mysterious, heavy, basic, neutral
- white: light, cool, snow, cleanliness, purity, clean, sterling, innocent, silent, inexplicable, normality, life
- neutral gray: quality, quiet, classic, inertia, ashes, passion, practical, timeless, old age, cunning, cool
- earth-tone red: warm, wholesome, welcome, good, healthy, fit, sound
- mid-range pink-red: restrained, toned down, soft, subdued, quiet, sentimental, sober, tame, domestic
- dark red: rich, elegant, refined, taste, expensive, mature
- pastel green: empathy, innate, completely, calm, quiet, smoothing, natural, sympathy, compassion

Color Scheme: direct complementary with shading plus neutrals

Incredible in its design and concept, this CD package becomes an interactive toy, creating a multitude of metamorphosing images. Destined to be a collector's item, this design is truly a masterpiece.

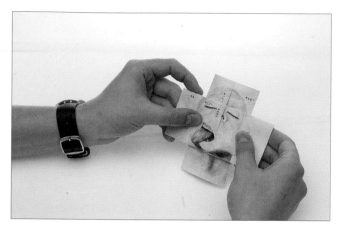

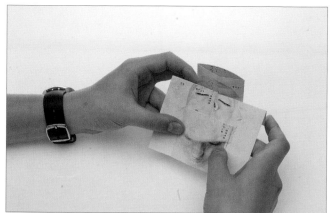

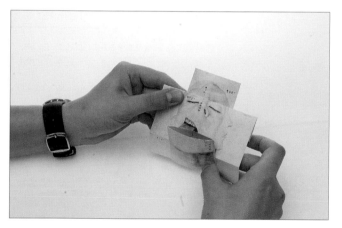

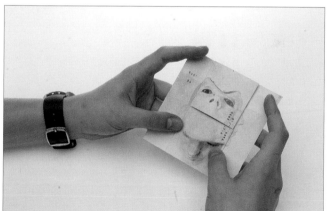

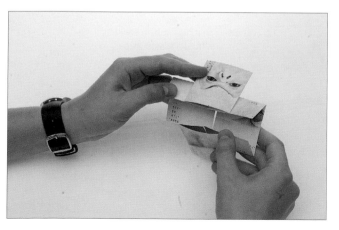

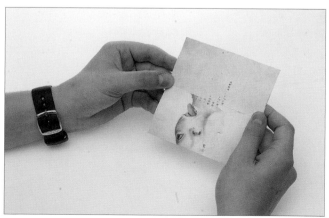

THE PRIVATE PRESS

Designer: Gabriela Lopez De Dennis

Associative Color Response:

- high-chroma orange: producing, healing, tasty, growing, fire, warm, cleanliness, cheerfulness
- high-chroma blue: dignity, spaciousness, sobriety, calm, height, lively, pleasing, rich
- earth-tone red: warm, wholesome, welcome, good, healthy, fit, sound
- high-chroma yellow-orange: enterprise, drive, target, goal, luxuriance, cheer, joy, fun, excitement, stimulates
- black: spatial, powerful, elegant, mysterious, heavy, basic, neutral

Color Scheme: near complementary with shading plus neutral

This CD package design fuses a multitude of illustration styles into a superb collage. The detail found in the composite front-cover image is fascinating when juxtaposed with its counterpart on the back. The opposition of form found between the front and back is what makes this package design so interesting to look at.

ROCK TOCUS

Studio: The Grafiosi
Art Director/Designer: Pushkar Thakur

Associative Color Response:

- black: spatial, powerful, elegant, mysterious, heavy, basic, neutral
- high-chroma blue: dignity, spaciousness, sobriety, calm, height, lively, pleasing, rich
- high-chroma green: life, use, motion, ebbing of life, springtime, infancy, wilderness, hope, peace
- high-chroma yellow-orange: enterprise, drive, target, goal, luxuriance, cheer, joy, fun, excitement, stimulates
- mid-range pink-red: restrained, toned down, soft, subdued, quiet, sentimental, sober, tame, domestic

Color Scheme: incongruous

Reminiscent of 1960s psychedelic designs, this CD cover uses a modular system (copying and pasting) to create an illustrative pattern made from the individual band members.

PALMISTRY

Studio: Alian Design
Art Director/Designer: Ian Shimkoviak

Associative Color Response:

- high-chroma red: surging, sexy, brilliant, intense, energizing, dramatic, stimulating
- mid-range pink-red: restrained, toned down, soft, subdued, quiet, sentimental, sober, tame, domestic
- mid-range orange: gentle, entice, good spirits, glad, nurturing, soft, fuzzy, delicious, fruity, sweet, inviting
- high-chroma orange: producing, healing, tasty, growing, fire, warm, cleanliness, cheerfulness
- high-chroma yellow-orange: enterprise, drive, target, goal, luxuriance, cheer, joy, fun, excitement, stimulates
- high-chroma blue: dignity, spaciousness, sobriety, calm, height, lively, pleasing, rich

Color Scheme: near complementary

The near complementary color combination with high-chroma hues creates a truly dynamic box design. The color palette coupled with the graphics not only make this design stand out from its competitors, but also make the product explode off the shelf.

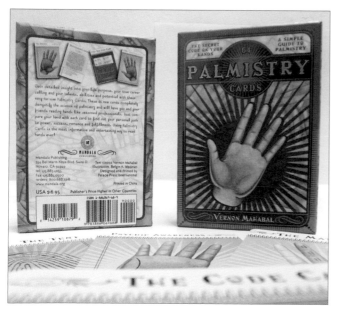

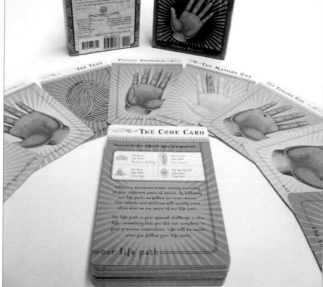

I AM IMAGINATION

Studio: Gouthier Design: a brand collective
Creative Director: Jonathan Gouthier
Designers: Gouthier Design Creative Team

Associative Color Response:

- black: spatial, powerful, elegant, mysterious, heavy, basic, neutral
- earth-tone red: warm, wholesome, welcome, good, healthy, fit, sound
- high-chroma orange: producing, healing, tasty, growing, fire, warm, cleanliness, cheerfulness
- high-chroma green-yellow: new growth, lemony, tart, fruity, acidic
- high-chroma green: life, use, motion, ebbing of life, springtime, infancy, wilderness, hope, peace
- dark green: nature, mountains, lakes, natural, mature growth, versatility, traditional, money, trustworthy, refreshing

Color Scheme: near complementary plus black

Fifteen local ad. agencies were asked to put their ideas on a foam head, which was then photographed and used for marketing.

MOCAFÉ

Studio: Mary Hutchison Design LLC
Art Director/Designer:
Mary Chin Hutchison

Associative Color Response:

- earth-tone red: warm, wholesome, welcome, good, healthy, fit, sound
- high-chroma orange: producing, healing, tasty, growing, fire, warm, cleanliness, cheerfulness
- high-chroma yellow-orange: enterprise, drive, target, goal, luxuriance, cheer, joy, fun, excitement, stimulates
- high-chroma yellow-green: lemony, tart, fruity, acidic, sharp, bold, trendy, strength, sunlight, biology
- high-chroma green: life, use, motion, ebbing of life, springtime, infancy, wilderness, hope, peace
- pastel blue: pleasure, calm, quiet, hygienic, peaceful, refreshing, clean, cool, water, heavenly

Appetite Rating:

- high-chroma orange: excellent
- high-chroma yellow-orange: excellent
- high-chroma yellow-green: excellent
- high-chroma green: excellent
- pastel blue: excellent

Associative Taste:

- high-chroma orange: producing, healing, tasty, growing, fire, warm, cleanliness, cheerfulness
- high-chroma orange: very sweet
- high-chroma yellow-orange: very sweet
- high-chroma yellow-green: very sweet, lemony

Color Scheme: near complementary

This package design series is a great example of color-coding. Note how the graphics and typography are basically the same, and only the lower color bar changes from vessel to vessel.

CHARLIE & THE CHOCOLATE FACTORY

Studio: Nita B. Creative
Art Director: Renita Breitenbucher
Designers: Renita Breitenbucher,
Kimberly Welter
Illustrator: Quentin Blake

Associative Color Response:

- high-chroma green: life, use, motion, ebbing of life, springtime, infancy, wilderness, hope, peace
- high-chroma reddish-purple: sweet taste, subtle, restlessness, prolongs life, feminine elegance, tender longing
- high-chroma blue: dignity, spaciousness, sobriety, calm, height, lively, pleasing, rich
- high-chroma yellow: energy, anticipation, agreeable, pleasant, welcome, vigorous, noble, youthful
- high-chroma orange: producing, healing, tasty, growing, fire, warm, cleanliness, cheerfulness
- mid-range orange: gentle, entice, good spirits, glad, nurturing, soft, fuzzy, delicious, fruity, sweet, inviting

Color Scheme: incongruous

Each holiday season, Marshall Field's creates a themed display in its stores in downtown Chicago and Minneapolis, and these have become an annual destination for thousands of families and tourists. Field's wanted to create a product line to sell in conjunction with their 2003 holiday theme, "Charlie and the Chocolate Factory." A bright, energetic color palette and original illustrations by Quentin Blake, of confections and Chocolate Factory characters, were used to bring the "Charlie" product line to life. As this line was varied, careful attention was made to the production of each piece and how color was applied. Because of Quentin Blake's vibrant and intricate watercolor illustrations, most of the product and packaging was printed in 4-color process. Other applications that required individual PMS colors—threads for the apron and caps, and inks on the soap-on-a-rope—were also given careful consideration.

MARSHALL FIELD'S

Art Director/Designer/Illustrator:
Renita Breitenbucher
Studio: Nita B. Creative

Associative Color Response:

- high-chroma red: surging, brilliant, intense, energizing, sexy, dramatic, stimulating
- high-chroma reddish-purple: sweet taste, subtle, restlessness, prolongs life, feminine elegance, tender longing
- high-chroma purple: celibacy, rage, deep, nostalgia, memories, power, spirituality, infinity, dignified
- dark green: nature, mountains, lakes, natural, mature growth, versatility, traditional, money, trustworthy, refreshing
- pastel green: empathy, innate, completely, calm, quiet, smoothing, natural, sympathy, compassion

Appetite Rating:

- high-chroma red: excellent
- high-chroma reddish-purple: excellent
- high-chroma purple: excellent
- dark green: good
- pastel green: excellent

Associative Taste:

- high-chroma red: very sweet

Color Scheme: direct complementary

Candy canes, sugar plums, gingerbread houses: candy and confections are a part of the Christmas season, so Marshall Field's developed a line of candies and gifts not only to grace the holidays, but also to satisfy the palates of those who had just toured the store's 2003 "Charlie & the Chocolate Factory" holiday exhibit. The packaging was given playful colors and candy shapes that coordinated perfectly with the merchandise, while maintaining Marshall Field's unmistakable brand.

IMAGEÓDESIGN

Studio: Twointandem
Art Directors/Designers: Sanver Kanidinc, Elena Ruano Kanidinc

Associative Color Response:

- high-chroma green-yellow: new growth, lemony, tart, fruity, acidic
- high-chroma yellow-green: lemony, tart, fruity, acidic, sharp, bold, trendy, strength, sunlight, biology
- high-chroma purple: celibacy, rage, deep, nostalgia, memories, power, spirituality, infinity, dignified
- high-chroma reddish-purple: sweet taste, subtle, restlessness, prolongs life, feminine elegance, tender longing

Color Scheme: direct complementary/ near complementary

A conceptual piece, with this neat, clean kit Twointandem introduced their new Imageódesign. The business card lists their services, inviting clients to freshen up their look while reinforcing the promotional message. Inspired by bath products (a daisy-shaped bar of soap and a shower cap are found inside), they played off the opposite—stinky, old, tired, and stale. Numerous empirical tests were conducted to find the most refreshing combinations of scents, colors, and shapes.

VIVIL

Studio: Solutions
Creative Director: Micha Goes
Designer: Andi Friedl

Associative Color Response:

- high-chroma red: surging, sexy, brilliant, intense, energizing, dramatic, stimulating
- high-chroma yellow-orange: enterprise, drive, target, goal, luxuriance, cheer, joy, fun, excitement, stimulates
- pastel pink: soft, sweet, tender, cute, comfortable, snug, rarefied, delicate, female babies, delicate, cozy, subtle
- high-chroma green-yellow: new growth, lemony, tart, fruity, acidic
- high-chroma green: life, use, motion, ebbing of life, springtime, infancy, wilderness, hope, peace
- dark green: nature, mountains, lakes, natural, mature growth, versatility, traditional, money, trustworthy, refreshing

Appetite Rating:

- high-chroma red: excellent
- high-chroma yellow-orange: excellent
- pastel pink: excellent
- high-chroma green-yellow: excellent
- high-chroma green: excellent
- dark green: good

Associative Taste:

- high-chroma red: very sweet
- high-chroma yellow-orange: very sweet
- pastel pink: sweet

Color Scheme: direct complementary with tinting

This Vivil package design takes advantage of intense high-chroma hues to increase the consumer's emotive response.

ZUMMER

Studio: Midnite Oil
Art Director/Designer:
Mongkolsri Janjarasskul

Associative Color Response:
- high-chroma red: surging, brilliant, intense, energizing, sexy, dramatic
- pastel pink: soft, sweet, tender, cute, comfortable, snug, rarefied, delicate, female babies, delicate, cozy, subtle
- high-chroma green-yellow: new growth, lemony, tart, fruity, acidic
- high-chroma green: life, use, motion, ebbing of life, springtime, infancy, wilderness, hope, peace
- black: spatial, powerful, elegant, mysterious, heavy, basic, neutral

Appetite Rating:
- high-chroma red: excellent
- pastel pink: excellent
- high-chroma green-yellow: excellent
- high-chroma green: excellent
- black: excellent

Associative Taste:
- high-chroma red: very sweet
- pastel pink: sweet

Color Scheme: direct complementary plus neutral

The original Zummer logo and motif utilized traditional Chinese brushwork. This design incorporates an Oriental watercolor approach to portray a fresh look while maintaining brand recognition.

NESTLÉ (THAI) LTD.

Designer: FiF DESIGN House Team

Associative Color Response:
- high-chroma yellow-orange: enterprise, drive, target, goal, luxuriance, cheer, joy, fun, excitement, stimulates
- pastel yellow: pleasant, sunshine, glad, compassionate, tender, kindhearted, cheerful
- golden-yellow/beige: dignified, pleasant, autumn, flowers, harvest, rich, sun
- high-chroma red: surging, sexy, brilliant, intense, energizing, dramatic, stimulating
- high-chroma green-yellow: new growth, lemony, tart, fruity, acidic
- high-chroma blue: poor to good

Appetite Rating:
- high-chroma yellow-orange: excellent
- pastel yellow: poor to good
- golden-yellow/beige: good to excellent
- high-chroma red: excellent
- high-chroma green-yellow: excellent
- high-chroma blue: poor to good

Associative Taste:
- high-chroma yellow-orange: very sweet
- pastel yellow: sweet
- high-chroma red: very sweet

Color Scheme: analogous plus primary hues

As can be seen in this packaging, ergonomics plays an important role in package design. The design of the tin can fits ergonomically in the palm of the hand.

GODIVA CHOCOLATIER

Art Director: John T. Drew
Designer: Lydia Adi

Associative Color Response:
- earth-tone red: warm, wholesome, welcome, good, healthy, fit, sound
- earth tone: delicious, deep, rich, warm, life, work, wholesome
- dark orange: exhilarating, inspiring, stirring, stimulating, moving, provoking
- mid-range orange: gentle, entice, good spirits, glad, nurturing, soft, fuzzy, delicious, fruity, sweet, inviting
- high-chroma green-yellow: new growth, lemony, tart, fruity, acidic

Appetite Rating:
- earth tone: good
- mid-range orange: good to excellent
- high-chroma green-yellow: excellent

Associative Taste:
- mid-range orange: sweet

Color Scheme: near complementary

The conceptual strategy for this design was based on the multitude of flavors well-crafted chocolates can provide. A visual metaphorical representation of this phenomenon is layered graphically on the cover of the tin.

LIP GLAZE

Art Director: John T. Drew
Designer: Sara Abdi

Associative Color Response:
- black: spatial, powerful, elegant, mysterious, heavy, basic, neutral
- high-chroma blue: dignity, spaciousness, sobriety, calm, height, lively, pleasing, rich
- mid-range pink-red: restrained, toned down, soft, subdued, quiet, sentimental, sober, tame, domestic
- high-chroma yellow-orange: enterprise, drive, target, goal, luxuriance, cheer, joy, fun, excitement, stimulates
- pastel blue: pleasure, calm, quiet, hygienic, peaceful, refreshing, clean, cool, water, heavenly

Color Scheme: two points of a tetrad

A high-contrast, pushed image is used to visually separate the lip glaze from the female model. An indexical reference of the glaze is used repeatedly in different sizes to reinforce the content.

BOLS

Studio: 1972dg
Art Director/Designer: Carlos Marques

Associative Color Response:

• dark red: rich, elegant, refined, taste, expensive, mature
• high-chroma orange: producing, healing, tasty, growing, fire, warm, cleanliness, cheerfulness
• mid-range orange: gentle, good spirits, glad, nurturing, soft, fuzzy, delicious, fruity, sweet, inviting
• high-chroma yellow-orange: enterprise, drive, target, goal, luxuriance, cheer, joy, fun, excitement, stimulates
• pastel blue: pleasure, calm, quiet, hygienic, peaceful, refreshing, clean, cool, water, heavenly
• black: spatial, powerful, elegant, mysterious, heavy, basic, neutral

Appetite Rating:
• high-chroma orange: excellent
• mid-range orange: good to excellent
• high-chroma yellow-orange: excellent
• pastel blue: excellent
• black: excellent

Associative Taste:
• high-chroma orange: very sweet
• mid-range orange: sweet
• high-chroma yellow-orange: very sweet

Color Scheme: direct complementary

An explosion of hue, this package design uses overprinting to achieve a multitude of colors. Typography is employed as image to create a bold flat-pattern illustration.

ART KIT

Art Director/Designer/Illustrator:
Renita Breitenbucher
Studio: Nita B. Creative

Associative Color Response:

• high-chroma blue: dignity, spaciousness, sobriety, calm, height, lively, pleasing, rich
• high-chroma reddish-purple: sweet taste, subtle, restlessness, prolongs life, feminine elegance, tender longing
• pastel green: empathy, innate, completely, calm, quiet, smoothing, natural, sympathy, compassion
• high-chroma green: life, use, motion, ebbing of life, springtime, infancy, wilderness, hope, peace
• high-chroma red: surging, brilliant, intense, energizing, sexy, dramatic, stimulating
• mid-range pink-red: restrained, toned down, soft, subdued, quiet, sentimental, sober, tame, domestic
• high-chroma pink: stimulates, aggressive, genial, exciting, happy, high, fun, excitement, attention-getting, promising
• golden-yellow/beige: dignified, pleasant, autumn, flowers, harvest, rich, sun

Color Scheme: direct complementary

For this package a high-chroma direct complementary color palette is used to take advantage of their color associations and/or learned behavioral effects. A crude childlike illustration style and typography complements the color palette.

PADDYWAX: JOURNEY OF THE BEE

Studio: Principle
Art Director: Pamela Zuccker
Designer: Ally Gerson
Photographer: Kara Brennan © 2007

Associative Color Response:

- high-chroma green-yellow: new growth, lemony, tart, fruity, acidic
- gold: warm, opulent, expensive, radiant, valuable, prestigious
- earth tone: delicious, deep, rich, warm, life, work, wholesome
- high-chroma blue: dignity, spaciousness, sobriety, calm, height, lively, pleasing, rich
- high-chroma red: surging, sexy, brilliant, intense, energizing, dramatic, stimulating
- neutral gray: quality, quiet, classic, inertia, ashes, passion, practical, timeless, old age, cunning, cool
- high-chroma yellow-orange: enterprise, drive, target, goal, luxuriance, cheer, joy, fun, excitement, stimulates

Color Scheme: incongruous

Each fragrance in this line reflects a stop that a bee would make on its journey from the early blossoms of sweet clover to the raw honey in their hive. Each box boasts a modern sensibility, from the crisp black-and-white honeycomb pattern on the lid to the whimsical gold-foiled flight pattern that is revealed on the glossy, colored box when opened. The glass is matte black with a gold-foiled bee, and is hand poured with a honey-colored beeswax blend.

CHARLIE'S NOTES

Studio: Nita B. Creative
Art Director: Renita Breitenbucher
Designers: Renita Breitenbucher, Kimberly Welter
Illustrator: Quentin Blake

Associative Color Response:

- golden-yellow/beige: dignified, pleasant, autumn, flowers, harvest, rich, sun
- high-chroma orange: producing, healing, tasty, growing, fire, warm, cleanliness, cheerfulness
- high-chroma red: surging, sexy, brilliant, intense, energizing, dramatic, stimulating
- pastel blue: pleasure, calm, quiet, hygienic, peaceful, refreshing, clean, cool, water, heavenly
- high-chroma blue: dignity, spaciousness, sobriety, calm, height, lively, pleasing, rich

Color Scheme: direct complementary

An intense color palette softened with a pastel blue creates a natural backdrop for the childlike illustrations and typography. Packaging this product as a "lunch box"—something young children can associate with—is an excellent marketing strategy.

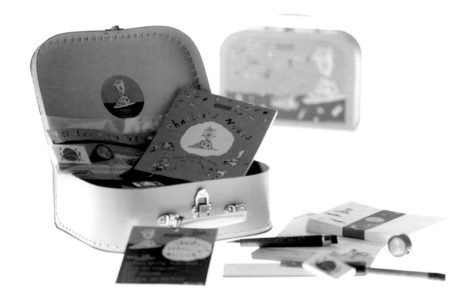

HEINZ HERITAGE

Studio: Wallace Church
Creative Director: Stan Church

Associative Color Response:

- gold: warm, opulent, expensive, radiant, valuable, prestigious
- high-chroma blue: dignity, spaciousness, sobriety, calm, height, lively, pleasing, rich
- high-chroma red: surging, sexy, brilliant, intense, energizing, dramatic, stimulating
- high-chroma green: life, use, motion, ebbing of life, springtime, infancy, wilderness, hope, peace
- black: spatial, powerful, elegant, mysterious, heavy, basic, neutral

Appetite Rating:

- gold: excellent
- high-chroma blue: poor to good
- high-chroma red: excellent
- high-chroma green: excellent
- black: excellent

Associative Taste:

- high-chroma red: very sweet

Color Scheme: primaries plus neutral

H.J. Heinz Company, the king of ketchup, has marketed dozens of products under the Heinz brand for over 100 years. These used inconsistent and dated expressions of the Heinz identity and, as a result, they were getting lost on shelf and denigrating overall brand perception. Heinz consulted with Wallace Church to revive its "heritage" brands. A visual position was created around the brand's "tried-and-true" essence. Leveraging the brand's unique authenticity and recasting the message in a contemporary context was required. A more prominent logo and enhanced "keystone" shape highlight the Heinz brand, while consistent form and flavor "staging areas" enable consumers to quickly identify products. This architecture is applied consistently across the entire brand franchise, helping to elevate these products to the "icon" status that its ketchup enjoys.

THE VINES OF ILOK

Studio: International
Art Director/Designer: Boris Ljubicic

Associative Color Response:

- black: spatial, powerful, elegant, mysterious, heavy, basic, neutral
- high-chroma yellow-orange: enterprise, drive, target, goal, luxuriance, cheer, joy, fun, excitement, stimulates
- high-chroma orange: producing, healing, tasty, growing, fire, warm, cleanliness, cheerfulness
- pastel yellow: pleasant, sunshine, glad, compassionate, tender, kindhearted, cheerful
- dark red: rich, elegant, refined, taste, expensive, mature
- pastel blue: pleasure, calm, quiet, hygienic, peaceful, refreshing, clean, cool, water, heavenly
- black: spatial, powerful, elegant, mysterious, heavy, basic, neutral

Appetite Rating:

- black: excellent
- high-chroma yellow-orange: excellent
- high-chroma orange: excellent
- pastel yellow: poor to good
- pastel blue: excellent
- black: excellent

Associative Taste:

- high-chroma yellow-orange: very sweet
- high-chroma orange: very sweet
- pastel yellow: sweet

Color Scheme: analogous plus neutral

The mountains of Ilok with their beautiful vineyards were the inspiration for this package design. Color coding was used to establish different product lines while the same typography and imagery work consistently throughout.

CALIFORNIA SUNSHINE

Studio: REFLECTUR.COM
Art Director/Designer: Gwendolyn Hicks

Associative Color Response:
- high-chroma red: surging, brilliant, intense, energizing, sexy, dramatic, stimulating
- earth-tone red: warm, wholesome, welcome, good, healthy, fit, sound
- high-chroma orange: producing, healing, tasty, growing, fire, warm, cleanliness, cheerfulness
- high-chroma green-yellow: new growth, lemony, tart, fruity, acidic
- mid-range red-purple: charming, elegant, select, refined, subtle, nostalgic, delicate, sweet scented, floral, sweet taste
- pastel blue: pleasure, calm, quiet, hygienic, peaceful, refreshing, clean, cool, water, heavenly
- black: spatial, powerful, elegant, mysterious, heavy, basic, neutral

Appetite Rating:
- high-chroma red: excellent
- high-chroma orange: excellent
- high-chroma green-yellow: excellent
- mid-range red-purple: good
- pastel blue: excellent
- black: excellent

Associative Taste:
- high-chroma red: very sweet
- high-chroma orange: very sweet
- mid-range red-purple: sweet

Color Scheme: incongruous

These beautiful rural illustrations are majestic in their execution, reminiscent of the orange-crate labels from southern California in the 1920s.

5 CALIFORNIA BLOSSOMS

Art Director: John T. Drew
Designer: Michael Stapleton

Associative Color Response:
- mid-range pink-red: restrained, toned down, soft, subdued, quiet, sentimental, sober, tame, domestic
- pastel pink: soft, sweet, tender, cute, comfortable, snug, rarefied, delicate, female babies, delicate, cozy, subtle
- high-chroma reddish-purple: sweet taste, subtle, restlessness, prolongs life, feminine elegance, tender longing
- high-chroma orange: producing, healing, tasty, growing, fire, warm, cleanliness, cheerfulness
- high-chroma yellow-orange: enterprise, drive, target, goal, luxuriance, cheer, joy, fun, excitement, stimulates
- high-chroma yellow: anticipation, agreeable, pleasant, welcome, vigorous, noble, youthful energy
- high-chroma purple: celibacy, rage, deep, nostalgia, memories, power, spirituality, infinity, dignified
- high-chroma bluish-purple: meditative, restlessness, expensive, regal, classic, powerful, tender, longing, elegant
- high-chroma blue: dignity, spaciousness, sobriety, calm, height, lively, pleasing, rich
- black: spatial, powerful, elegant, mysterious, heavy, basic, neutral

Color Scheme: analogous

The modular illustrations—each illustration is made from one or two parts, copied, pasted, and scaled up or down—are beautifully executed with high-chroma colors and flat patterns. The die cut for the exterior package is cleverly conceived by indexically referencing a bee, helping to place the package design in context.

PURE & NATURAL

Studio: Midnite Oil
Art Director/Designer:
Mongkolsri Janjarasskul

Associative Color Response:

- pastel green: empathy, innate, calm, quiet, smoothing, natural, sympathy, compassion
- neutral gray: quality, quiet, classic, inertia, ashes, passion, practical, timeless, old age, cunning, cool
- dark gray: wise, cultured, mature, professional, classic, expensive, sophisticated, solid, enduring,
- high-chroma red: surging, sexy, brilliant, intense, energizing, dramatic, stimulating

- high-chroma orange: producing, healing, tasty, growing, fire, warm, cleanliness, cheerfulness

Color Scheme: near complementary plus neutrals

Pure & Natural is a series of cosmetics from in2it, which contain ingredients including fruit and vegetable extracts. Transparent packaging substrates were used so that the consumer could see the slices of different fruits suspended within the product.

VIDA ORGÁNICA

Studio: Estudio Iuvaro
Art Director: Cecilia Iuvaro
Designers: Mariano Gioia,
Sebastián Yáñez

Associative Color Response:

- black: spatial, powerful, elegant, mysterious, heavy, basic, neutral
- mid-range red-purple: charming, elegant, select, refined, subtle, nostalgic, delicate, sweet scented, floral, sweet taste
- high-chroma orange: producing, healing, tasty, growing, fire, warm, cleanliness, cheerfulness
- high-chroma green-yellow: new growth, lemony, tart, fruity, acidic
- dark green: nature, mountains, lakes, natural, mature growth, versatility, traditional, money, trustworthy, refreshing
- dark orange: exhilarating, inspiring, stirring, stimulating, moving, provoking

Appetite Rating:

- black: excellent
- mid-range red-purple: good
- high-chroma orange: excellent
- high-chroma green-yellow: excellent
- dark green: good
- dark orange: poor

Associative Taste:

- mid-range red-purple: sweet
- high-chroma orange: very sweet

Color Scheme: near triad plus neutral

Vida Orgánica is the only wine belonging to the Familia Zuccardi Vineyard that is made from organically cultivated grapevines. The packaging has been redesigned while paying homage to the original design by Estudio Iuvaro. The redesign objective was to incorporate a wider use of color in order to differentiate the varietals from one another and to produce a greater impact in the market place.

EXPECT

Art Director/Designer: Chapman Tse

Associative Color Response:
- black: spatial, powerful, elegant, mysterious, heavy, basic, neutral
- gold: warm, opulent, expensive, radiant, valuable, prestigious
- high-chroma green: life, use, motion, ebbing of life, springtime, infancy, wilderness, hope, peace

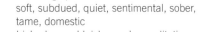

- high-chroma yellow-orange: joy, fun, enterprise, drive, target, goal, luxuriance, excitement, stimulates
- dark orange: exhilarating, inspiring, stirring, stimulating, moving, provoking
- high-chroma orange: producing, healing, tasty, growing, fire, warm, cleanliness, cheerfulness

Appetite Rating:
- black: excellent
- gold: excellent
- high-chroma green: excellent
- high-chroma yellow-orange: excellent
- high-chroma orange: excellent

Associative Taste:
- high-chroma yellow-orange: very sweet
- high-chroma orange: very sweet

Color Scheme: incongruous/achromatic

This near achromatic color scheme uses warm accent hues to separate the tea leaves and product name.

LEMON TATTOO

Studio: SandorMax
Designer: Zoltan Csillag

Associative Color Response:
- high-chroma yellow: anticipation, agreeable, pleasant, welcome, vigorous, noble, youthful energy

- mid-range pink-red: restrained, toned down, soft, subdued, quiet, sentimental, sober, tame, domestic
- high-chroma bluish-purple: meditative, restlessness, expensive, regal, classic, powerful, tender, longing, elegant
- high-chroma green-yellow: new growth, lemony, tart, fruity, acidic
- pastel blue: pleasure, calm, quiet, hygienic, peaceful, refreshing, clean, cool, water, heavenly

Appetite Rating:
- high-chroma yellow: good
- mid-range pink-red: good
- high-chroma bluish-purple: excellent
- high-chroma green-yellow: excellent
- pastel blue: excellent

Associative Taste:
- high-chroma yellow: very sweet
- mid-range pink-red: sweet

Color Scheme: two points of a triad

Texture is a visual magnet, and here Lemon Tattoo uses it to the fullest extent. By employing this technique, an aged appearance is immediately established, promoting longevity within the marketplace.

PADDYWAX CLASSIC

Studio: Principle
Art Director/Designer: Pamela Zuccker
Photographer: David Lefler © 2007

Associative Color Response:

- high-chroma blue: dignity, spaciousness, sobriety, calm, height, lively, pleasing, rich
- high-chroma red: surging, sexy, brilliant, intense, energizing, dramatic, stimulating
- high-chroma yellow-green: lemony, tart, fruity, acidic, sharp, bold, trendy, strength, sunlight, biology
- black: spatial, powerful, elegant, mysterious, heavy, basic, neutral
- earth-tone red: warm, wholesome, welcome, good, healthy, fit, sound
- dark green: nature, mountains, lakes, natural, mature growth, versatility, traditional, money, trustworthy, refreshing

Color Scheme: near triad

Paddywax needed to reestablish a bold presence in their core product line, and Principle was brought in to develop new packaging and point-of-sale materials. The old packaging left them susceptible to being perceived as "country." To address this, the designer came up with a preppy-chic identity system that combined classic black-and-white stitched ribbon with colorful stripes and solids to reflect the intense color palette of the wax. Tubular packaging was updated with a sophisticated, rigid box that, when separated, exposes the signature stripe pattern. The result was a whole new look and feel that will drive future design and communications decisions.

SMS

Studio: International
Art Director/Designer/Photography/Illustrator:
Boris Ljubicic

Associative Color Response:

- neutral gray: quality, quiet, classic, inertia, ashes, passion, practical, timeless, old age, cunning, cool
- high-chroma red: surging, sexy, brilliant, intense, energizing, dramatic, stimulating
- dark red: rich, elegant, refined, taste, expensive, mature
- high-chroma orange: producing, healing, tasty, growing, fire, warm, cleanliness, cheerfulness
- mid-green: warlike, forces, safari, military, camouflaged, classic

Appetite Rating:

- neutral gray: poor to good
- high-chroma red: excellent
- high-chroma orange: excellent
- mid-green: excellent

Associative Taste:

- high-chroma red: very sweet
- high-chroma orange: very sweet

Color Scheme: analogous plus neutral and tinting

Surely no one has ever eaten jam without getting his or her hands sticky? The conceptual strategy for this piece is based on that assumption. SMS Jams are high-quality delicatessen products that are "so tasty that we couldn't hide the evidence."

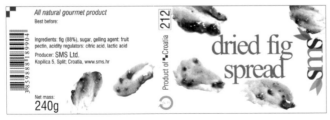

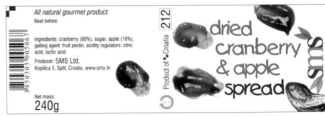

MARTHA STEWART EVERYDAY

Studio: Doyle Partners

Associative Color Response:

- blue-green: pristine, pure, serious, cleanliness, incorruptible, pensive, tranquillity, lively
- high-chroma red: surging, sexy, brilliant, intense, energizing, dramatic, stimulating
- neutral gray: quality, quiet, classic, inertia, ashes, passion, practical, timeless, old age, cunning, cool
- high-chroma orange: producing, healing, tasty, growing, fire, warm, cleanliness, cheerfulness
- golden-yellow/beige: dignified, pleasant, autumn, flowers, harvest, rich, sun
- black: spatial, powerful, elegant, mysterious, heavy, basic, neutral
- high-chroma blue: dignity, spaciousness, sobriety, calm, height, lively, pleasing, rich

Color Scheme: analogous plus neutral, near complementary plus neutral with shading and tinting, and incongruous plus neutral with shading and tinting

The Martha Stewart Everyday system is designed with a simple logo and an overall clarity that is synonymous with the brand, delivered in a wide assortment of bold colors and accessible type. This crisp, colorful packaging provides a cohesive, unifying effect

for products in many different categories. Packaging was constructed to highlight the product attributes, allowing light to shine through the glassware packages, letting customers feel the weight of flatware, or even presenting uninterrupted surfaces of plates in a subtle range of colors—all conceived to give customers a better understanding of the design properties of the products.

Glossary

absorbed light: light that is absorbed by an object; the opposite of transmitted light. The lightwaves absorbed by an object are transformed into heat. The darker the color, the more waves are absorbed and thus the more heat it produces.

achromatic: hues made from black, gray, and white.

additive color theory/mixing: combining lightwaves to create colors.

afterimage: illusions occurring when retinal cones and neurons become fatigued or overstimulated. Photoreceptor cells are responsible for human perception of color. A photoreceptor cell can become fatigued if it fixates on a particular color, and this will cause a false electrical impulse by the photoreceptor cell, thus creating the afterimage.

analogous colors: a color grouping in which the colors are to the near left and right of each other. An analogous color scheme is harmonious because all colors within the palette have a certain percentage of each other built into them.

aqueous coating: one of four basic types of coatings applied to packaging including varnish, UV coating, and laminates. Aqueous coating is, as the name implies, a resin- and water-based covering.

aseptic packaging: a method of extending shelf life through the elimination or control of unwanted organisms.

blind emboss: an emboss that is not registered to a printed image.

bronzing: an effect that develops when some inks are exposed to light and air that creates a false reading in the calculation of color. Bronzing causes a glare effect in 3D color space. Most often it occurs in inks that are warm in nature, or color builds that have

a mixture of warm and cool colors: the pigments in warm colors begin to rise up through the cooler ink pigments.

calibration: tuning an instrument or a device to obtain optimal results.

characterization: the determination of the color space needed by creating color profiles that help to simulate the gamut need for perceptual appearance—both individually and uniformly—throughout the working environment.

chroma: color intensity. Sometimes referred to as the color's brightness, chroma is another word for the Y tristimulus value in 3D color theory.

chromatic colors: a series of colors arranged in set increments.

color contrast: the difference between light-waves detected by the apparatus of the eyeball. The photoreceptive fields near and around the fovea are responsible for four kinds of vision: motion, form/silhouette, depth, and color. All four of these factors determine color contrast.

color mixing: the process by which different pigments, dyes, colorants, or lightwaves are mixed to create a new hue.

color profile: assignment of a working color space.

color purity: the absence of white, black, or gray from a hue.

color rendition: the phenomenon of two colors appearing the same in one light source, but very different in another.

color saturation: the richness of a hue. Color saturation is controlled by the amount of gray added to a particular hue and has a bearing on the intensity, or chroma, of a color.

color scheme: the color combinations selected for a particular design.

color shading: combining a color and black.

color temperature: the degree of warmth or coolness that a color suggests.

color tinting: adding a small amount of one color or white pigment to another color.

color toning: adding one complementary color to another.

color value: the relative lightness or darkness of the color as perceived by the mind's eye.

Color Value Differential (CVD): the difference between two hues as measured by the Y tristimulus value.

color wheel: a matrix composed of primary, secondary, and tertiary hues or colors.

color work flow: the management of color from device to device in the daily context of a working environment.

commercially sterile packaging: an aseptic method of packaging that does not eliminate all microorganisms, but eliminates the microorganisms' ability to reproduce under nonrefrigerated conditions.

complementary colors: hues that are found on opposite sides of the color wheel.

complex fields of vision: the mechanics of perceiving the location and orientation of an object. Complex fields help humans to interpret the shape, contour, and mass of an object.

complex subtractive mixing: the process of removing lightwaves through absorption and scattering. Complex subtractive mixing occurs when light bounces off an object and then is either reflected back in the direction of the viewer, absorbed by the object as heat, and/or scattered in various directions.

cones: the receptor cells responsible for our perception of bright light and color.

conversion: the uniform color optimization from one device to the other for the purpose of reproduction.

die cutting: one of the most common methods of engineering a score, perforation, or specialized cut for package design. Like a cookie cutter, dull and/or sharp steel rules are bent to the desired shape and then pressed into the paper.

dry trapped: printing over a dry ink.

early bind: the color space is assigned early in the process, and before it is sent to press.

electromagnetic radiation: the transfer of radiant energy as heat and light, through air, water, or vacuums. Electromagnetic radiation is produced by a light source, either artificial or natural.

embossing: the process whereby a metal die containing a relief image presses into the paper, creating a raised image. Debossing creates a lowered image through the same process.

engraving: a highly specialized technique used to create plates and dies for foil stamping or the intaglio and gravure printing processes.

expiration date: the point at which an edible product is no longer considered safe for consumption.

fixation points: discrete points at which the eye is in focus. The eye moves along the printed line in a succession of small, rapid jerks, from one point to another. These points are called fixation points, and it is only at these that the eye is in focus.

flood varnish: a varnish that is flooded across the whole surface of the substrate. Typically used to protect paper against scuffing and rubbing during handling or bulk processing.

foil stamping: a process whereby a thin layer of foil is adhered to the surface through the use of a heated plate or die that is stamped onto the surface of the substrate. Also known as hot stamping, dry stamping, flat stamping, leaf stamping, foil imprinting, leafing, and blocking.

fovea: a small spot on the retina that provides our narrow, central field of focused vision.

fugitive colors: colorants, pigments, or dyes that change or lose color rapidly when exposed to light and air.

glazing: the contrast created by a highly burnished blind emboss on textured paper. Glazing requires more pressure and heat, but creates outstanding contrast on dark stock.

gloss emboss: an emboss method that uses a clear foil to create a highly varnished effect on blind-embossed stock. Works best on light-colored stock.

gold leafing and gilding: the highly burnished metallic gold in illuminated manuscripts, paintings, etc.

hard proof: a physical hard copy pulled from a color printer or press.

harmonious colors: two or more colors that have a sameness about them.

harmony of analogous colors: of scale: color tones that are produced through a single scale; of hue: colors that have the same relative lightness to the mind's eye (color value rating); of dominant color: hues that are related to the factors involved in color contrast.

harmony of contrast: of scale—two colors with the same or near same color value rating, but different hues; of hue—chromatic colors with distinctly different color value ratings mixed together in stepped increments; of color temperature—two colors with the same or near same color value rating, but different color temperatures.

hermetically sealed packaging: packaging that is sealed airtight in an effort to exclude organisms from entering and to prevent gas or vapor from entering or exiting.

hue: a classified or specified color.

hypercomplex fields of vision: matrix fields of photoreceptor cells within the brain that respond most favorably to moving objects that behave with a set direction and definite position/pattern.

iconic information: a sign that bears a similarity or resemblance to the thing it signifies—it is what it is.

illuminant: light, physically realized or not, defined by spectral power distribution.

incongruous colors: colors that make a discordant combination. A color used with another hue that is to the right or left of its complement (for example, yellow-orange as one color and reddish-purple, or bluish-green as another) creates an incongruous combination. Incongruous combinations have one color that runs through each hue, and one that does not.

indexical information: a sign that arises by virtue of some sort of factual or casual connection with its object.

integrated sphere: a hollow sphere used to collect all of the light reflected from the surface of a color sample.

invariant pairs: color samples or objects having an identical spectral-reflectance curve and the same color coordinates. The phenomenon of invariant pairs means that, in 3D color mixing, colors match mathematically in all standard light sources, but they look different.

iris: the portion of the eye that helps to focus an image, adjust the amount of light passing through the pupil to define depth of field, and give eyes their color.

L*a*b* colors: model after the second stage of perceiving color within the human experience. The Commission Internationale de L'Eclairage (CIE) developed the (L*a*b*) system (L)ightness, red/green, value (A), and yellow/blue, value (B) that is device independent, meaning this system runs true. The system is not altered by any software or hardware application, and can act as a translator for color systems that are device dependent. CMYK is an example of a device-dependent color system.

laminate: one of four basic types of coatings applied to packaging, including varnish, aqueous coating, and UV coating. Laminates are plastics that are glued to the surface, thus providing the highest level of water resistance.

laser cutting: a highly accurate method of cutting highly complex cut shapes not suitable for die cutting.

late bind: the color space is assigned late in the process, and after it is sent to press.

light energy: light distinguished by the human eye as colors.

metallic inks: inks that have metal flakes suspended in the resin of the ink.

metameric pairs: pairs of colors with different spectral-reflectance curves (see spectral power distribution curve) that have the same appearance in one light source but not in another.

monochromatic colors: hues consisting of one color, including screen percentages of tints, shades, and combinations of tints and shades (see color tinting and color shading).

neutral color: a hue with a near equal screen percentage of one or more colors, including its complementary.

pack or packing: the container in which multiple packages are distributed.

packaging: the container or material that directly houses the consumer product.

parent colors: two or more hues that are used to create or build an array of colors.

primary colors: pure hues that create the foundation of all color spectrums. Subtractive primaries: cyan, magenta, and yellow; black is added to create a full color spectrum for print. Additive primaries: red, green, and blue.

primary container: the package that directly contains the product.

primary visual cortex: a portion of the brain located at the end of the visual pathway, devoted to the input for and interpretation of sight.

pupil: the pupil is the black point in the center of the eye through which light travels in order to strike the retina. It operates like the leaf shutter of a camera, opening and closing in a circular pattern.

retina: the region at the back of the eyeball where the ganglion cells, cones, and rods are located.

rods: photoreceptors responsible for night vision. Rods are highly sensitive to light and operate effectively in dim light. They are responsible for distinguishing blacks, grays, and variations of white, but do not distinguish color.

scattering: a phenomenon that occurs when light strikes an object with a rough surface, causing lightwaves to reflect in many directions.

secondary colors: a hue formed by adding equal amounts of two primary colors to one another.

secondary container: the container that houses the primary packaging barrier.

shelf life: the length of time a perishable product is considered viable (ie, nutritional and palatable).

shell gold: a mix of gum arabic and gold-leaf particles made into a cake and traditionally stored in shells by Medieval and Renaissance artists. Shell gold was often used to create the unburnished metallic gold in illuminated manuscripts, paintings, etc.

simple fields of vision: photoreceptive fields that are parallel to one another and work best with moving stimuli.

simple subtractive mixing: removing light-waves through the absorption process.

simultaneous contrast: a strobing effect resulting from the use of unequal portions of colors.

soft proof: a screen color proof.

spectral power distribution curve: the spectrum of color seen by the human eye; when combined this makes white light.

split complementary colors: two or more hues on or near the opposite sides of the color wheel.

spot varnish: a varnish applied in a specified area of a design.

standard observer: a set angle of observation that affects the response of normal color vision.

standard source: a light source for which the characteristics—wavelength, intensity, etc.—have been specified.

subtractive color mixing: the process of removing lightwaves or matter in physical space to create additional colors.

symbolic information: something that represents or suggests another by virtue of their relationship, association, conversion, or resemblance.

tertiary colors: colors produced by mixing equal amounts of a primary and a secondary color.

tertiary container: the container, distribution packaging, or pallet and wrappers that hold the primary and secondary containers for transport.

thermography: an economical option that simulates the effects of engraving without a die and in a shorter time. A heat-sensitive or ultraviolet (UV) resin is mixed into the ink. When the ink is printed and exposed to heat, the resin reacts, giving the image a raised surface similar to engraving.

transmitted light: light that is reflected.

transparent: if light travels through an object uninterrupted, the object is transparent.

tristimulus values: X, Y, and Z tristimulus values refer to the amount of light the eyes see from the three primaries—red, green, and blue—of 3D color theory. These values are determined by the power (light source) × the reflectance × the standard observer (the equivalent of normal color vision for humans). The three most typical standard light sources are Source A (tungsten filament lamp), Source D50 and/or D65 (US and European standards for average daylight), and Source CWF (fluorescent lighting).

undercolor addition (UCA): a method of adding color to improve image quality. In four-color process, small amounts of color added to the cyan plate (no more than 10 percent) will improve color density. Undercolor addition is achieved through the CMY plates, but the cyan plate is used most often as it is the least efficient primary of the three—yellow is the most efficient.

undercolor removal (UCR): a method of removing color to improve image quality. In four-color process printing, the removal of cyan, magenta, and yellow from the black shadow areas will compensate for ink build up by replacing it with black ink. Also called Gray Component Replacement (GCR).

UV coating: one of four basic types of coatings applied to packaging that include varnish, aqueous coating, and laminates. UV coatings are plastics that dry when exposed to UV light.

varnish: one of four basic types of coatings applied to packaging that include aqueous coating, UV coating, and laminates. A varnish is the ink vehicle without pigment.

visual pathway: the pathway from the eyes to the back of the brain, the primary visual cortex, to which the electrical impulses travel to be recognized and interpreted in the mind's eye, instantly and right side up.

warm colors: colors that give the appearance of an object being nearer the observer than it is. Warm colors are derived from yellow, red, and orange. Any hue composed of a majority of one or more of these colors is said to be warm, including half of all specified purples.

wavelength range: the visual range within which humans can distinguish the color spectrum.

Websafe Color Cube: an arrangement of the 216 hues, at 20 percent intervals, that can be depicted accurately with most common computer platforms. This includes black and white and their shades and tints (see color shades and color tints).

wet trap: printing over a wet ink.

Y tristimulus value: a mathematical representation of relative lightness to the mind's eye.

Index